TALES FROM THE COUCH:
Healing, Humor, and Finding Hope

Research, Interviews, and Lessons
Learned from Thousands of People

By
Dr. Tracy Riley

Licensed Clinical Social Worker
Doctor of Clinical Psychology
Speaker, Author, Mental Health Clinician

Tales From The Couch: Healing, Humor, and Finding Hope

Dr. Tracy Riley

Copyright © 2020

All Rights Reserved.

All right reserved. No part of this publication may be reproduced, distributed, or transmitted in any form or by any means, including photocopying, recording, or other electronic or mechanical methods, without the prior written permission from the author, except in the case of brief quotations embodied in critical reviews and certain other non-commercial uses permitted by copyright law.

First Printing: September 2020

ISBN: 978-1-7354637-2-8

Portions of this book were originally published elsewhere.

Dr. Tracy Riley

Tracy Riley Counseling

11555 Central Parkway, Suite 701

Jacksonville, Florida 32224

(904) 704-2527

www.tracyriley.com

Dr. Tracy Riley is available to speak at your business or conference event on a variety of topics. Call (904) 704-2527 for booking information.

Check out her other books:
https://www.tracyriley.com/books

Meet Dr. Tracy Riley

Dr. Tracy Riley grew up in Alabama, in a dysfunctional blended family of his, hers, and ours. As the youngest of 10, and after several years of abuse and neglect, she was placed into a group foster home for several years. Her story is one of triumph, overcoming tragedy and finding her way.

Dr. Tracy Riley began her education at Auburn University, obtaining a Bachelor's Degree in Social Work. She moved on to Florida State University, obtaining a Master's Degree, also in Social Work. Shortly thereafter, she became licensed as a Licensed Clinical Social Worker in Florida. Most recently, she obtained her doctorate in Clinical Psychology in 2018 and became licensed in New York.

Dr. Tracy Riley has built her entire career helping individuals, couples and families become the best versions of themselves. She has also worked with other mental health clinicians, sharing her wide knowledge base by teaching clinical skills and business courses.

Her work isn't magic, though the results of her efforts have been magical.

While building a successful business is a great goal to strive toward, Dr. Riley is most proud of her three adult children. Each of them have followed her footsteps in some way, embracing the mental health field.

Are you looking to create your own personal change, grow your business, or improve some aspect of your life? Would you like to bring Dr. Tracy Riley to your organization or conference as a keynote speaker? Contact her at (904) 704 2527 or visit www.tracyriley.com

Dedication and Acknowledgements

For Brittany, Brooke, and Wesley:

You've had the unfortunate opportunity to watch me make so many mistakes and you each could write your own book on that (please don't). Just know that despite fancy titles, degrees and all the success I have, the three of you are my greatest accomplishments. Without you, nothing else matters.

To my parents, who told me I wouldn't amount to anything, as well as other venom spewed at me, I proved you wrong. I did it in spite of you, and you get no credit other than teaching me what not to do as a parent.

In the last few years, so many individuals have inspired, encouraged, and guided my path. To Jason Kropidlowski, Rick Green, Jason Linett, Richard Clark, Dr. Richard Nongard, Sheila Granger, Karen Hand, James Hazlerig, Ken Guzzo, Michael DeSchalit, Mark Lakowske, Kevin Cole, Dr. Will Horton, Victoria Gallagher, Danny Candell, Cheryl and Larry Elman, and many others for welcoming a novice into the hypnosis community.

To Sara Hunt, Anna Wyke, Sabrina Bunn, Yolla Bailey, Lee Mikell, Lee Waters, Clinton McRay, Rebecca Felico, and the handful of clinicians before you, thank you for being a part of my team and growing with me and my practice.

To those who support, coach, and love my endeavors, Derrick Dorsey, Mark Missigman; the two of you are my biggest cheerleaders. To Marc Marshall—my friend, my proofreader, my listener, the one who always answers the phone—you are simply a gift.

To the individuals whose great stories I share here, while you will remain nameless—you are truly a gift. Thank you for sharing with and trusting me to keep your secrets safe.

Table of Contents

Chapter 1 Why Choose Therapy?...1
Chapter 2 Beaten But Not Broken..10
Chapter 3 10 Reasons to Talk to a Therapist 33
Chapter 4 Thoughts About Motherhood 38
Chapter 5 What Are The Rules?...45
Chapter 6 If A Man Wants You 56
Chapter 7 Teenage Pregnancy..59
Chapter 8 Balancing Work And Family: You Really Can Do It All!..62
Chapter 9 Give Me More...65
Chapter 10 The Gun Range 68
Chapter 11 Gentle Reminders 73
Chapter 12 Things I Have Learned While Being In 7th Grade As A 39-Year-Old Mom Of Three Teenagers..................76
Chapter 13 Positive Parenting--5 Surefire Ways to Improve Your Parenting Style...81
Chapter 14 Grief Dreams 90
Chapter 15 Eating Out With the Kids....Do You Dare? 92
Chapter 16 Marriage and Relationships...Is it Self or Service and are You Ready?..96
Chapter 17 One-Liners 99
Chapter 18 Are You Using Your Remote Control?.............. 107
Chapter 19 Live It, Own It, Act It 117
Chapter 20 Have You Ever Committed Suicide? 127
Chapter 21 It's a Wrap!.. 135

Chapter 1
Why Choose Therapy?

How does that make you feel? It's about as clichéd as it gets when it comes to talking about a therapist and what therapy is like. All good therapists will tell you it's also a line we *never* use. Okay, maybe not never; let's go with rarely. Because it is so clichéd, we just don't use it.

Why would someone choose therapy? It used to be that only "crazy" people went to counseling. There is also the thought that one must be seriously mentally ill in order to seek the services of a therapist. Over the years, I've heard creative names for therapy. It's been referred to as hocus pocus, mental brainwashing, head shrinking, and other, less printable terms. The truth is, people go to counseling for everyday normal life.

Research shows us that in the United States, an estimated 59 million people have received mental health treatment in the past two years and that 80% of those people found it effective. Chances are those numbers are even higher, as going to therapy isn't something one typically shares with their friends, family, co-workers, neighbors, etc. There's a stigma to mental health, and we will get to that at a later point.

Primary care physicians report that up to 80% of the ailments they see can be traced back to a mental health issue or concern. I don't use "mental health illness" because who says they go to the doctor for a "physical illness"? Usually, if one says they had a doctor's appointment, they are more specific about why, because there is no stigma in going to see a medical doctor for a physical issue or concern.

People attend therapy for a multitude of reasons. Trauma, such as a loss, is a common reason. It could be the loss of a loved one, loss of a job, disease, accident, divorce, etc. Life transition, such as marriage or moving, starting a new job, having a baby, is another common reason to seek therapy. Couples who want to improve their relationship will seek the help of a therapist, and some couples are required to attend premarital counseling in order to have their ceremony. Often times, a primary care doctor will refer their patients to a therapist for any of the reasons mentioned above.

Some people who attend therapy do so because of a severe mental illness. They want to get treatment for this, and to maintain their mental health. However, the majority of people who initiate counseling *do not* have a serious mental illness. They have life challenges, and I know we can all relate to that. I certainly can.

As a teenager, I had to attend therapy with my parents. We didn't talk to each other at home, so how in the world was I supposed to open up to a stranger, with my parents in the room? It was awkward, uncomfortable, and I hated every minute of it. However, I do remember one session in particular; my father was apologizing to me for all of the years of physical and emotional abuse he had put me through. The therapist encouraged me to look at him while he made his apologies. As a pre-teen, seeing my dad cry, as he apologizes for the atrocities towards me, is something that still lingers in my mind sometimes.

It would be great to say that life got better after that monumental breakthrough in the therapist's office that day. Unfortunately, that was not the case. Within a year or two, I was removed from my parents' care and put in a group foster home. I spent the next several years there, until I graduated high school. It's a story that very few people know, and even fewer people know the details. I will share some of those details in this book.

Maybe you've considered going to therapy at some point. Maybe you've wondered what it's like to "spill your guts" to a stranger. This book is a wonderful way to take the guesswork out of therapy. I will share my own unique approach to conducting therapy for the last 20+ years. I'll walk you through exactly what happens in my office. Once you are armed with knowledge and understanding, choosing to go to therapy is an easy process, one where you will benefit and things will only get better. With that being said, all therapists are different and my approach may not be the best one.

As a mental health clinician since 1999, I have had a wonderful career of helping people along their journeys. I have enjoyed almost every moment. Like all professions, there have been some not so good moments that caused me to question my career choice. However, a fellow social worker said it best; "Tracy, no matter what we are doing, we are social workers at heart. Whether it's agency work, private practice, or being a cashier at Publix, we are social workers, it's not what we do, it's who we are".

That comment has stuck with me for the last several years. I have always wanted to help people. I have sometimes helped people to my detriment, also known as a lack of boundaries, so yes, I am aware of and working on that!

People have a variety of reasons for choosing to go to counseling. But how do they determine who is the best counselor for them? Most people consider affordability first. Can they afford counseling? Almost every medical insurance carrier offers mental health benefits. Each plan differs, based on a multitude of factors; the contract with the employer, the geographical location, the specific healthcare plan, whether or not deductibles apply to out of pocket expenses.

After all, there is the expectation, which is incorrect, that they must go every single week for the rest of their lives in order to make improvements. While there are some people who remain in therapy for quite some time, not everyone needs ongoing assistance.

After affordability, people look for a counselor who specializes in their area of need. Beyond that, people make choices for a variety of reasons. Some people want proximity, or more years of experience. Some individuals request a particular type of counseling, or a specific degree. Whatever your criteria, it's like any other relationship; it's important to feel comfortable. After all, in order to get the most benefit, you'll be opening up and sharing your most personal secrets with this person.

As I mentioned, my first venture into counseling was because I was forced to go by the courts of Alabama. As a family, we attended counseling because of the abuse I was experiencing and to give my parents an opportunity to get the resources they could use to improve their parenting. While it didn't work out in that aspect, it did change my life. Prior to that, I had my heart set on being an English teacher, most likely for high-school-age kids. Because of my time with therapy, going to foster care, and being around social workers, I realized teaching wasn't my inclination after all.

I obtained my Bachelor's degree from Auburn University. Funny side note, I was four months pregnant with baby number three. It would be some time before I would put that education to good use. I received my Master's degree from Florida State University (as a single mom of three small kids). It wasn't until 13 years later that I finished the dream degree—a doctorate in Clinical Psychology. My mental health career has spanned over 20 years (I just dated myself and I feel old).

My current curriculum vitae is seven pages long, so I won't bore you with the details of that. However, I have worked in most aspects of social work. From starting an adoption agency, to building a private practice, to counseling inner-city youth after a homicide, I have been around the block—you know what I mean here. This book is put together with love, for laughter, and to learn how to live in our sometimes senseless world. It's a collection of blogs, blurbs, and anecdotes of things I have heard over the years.

Maybe you have considered seeing a therapist. You probably wonder what really goes on behind closed doors. Therapy isn't a scary thing, but it is one of the most narcissistic things we can do. We go and talk about ourselves for an hour. Who else will let you ramble on about yourself for that long? Neighbors, coworkers, family members, and friends all eventually get tired of listening and start talking about their own issues or problems.

Did you know that even therapists see a therapist? We have to. We have to maintain our mental health so we can better help those around us.

Why did I write this book? For several reasons really. The most important is to normalize seeing a therapist, to help take away the stigma of it. I want to let the reader see that going to therapy is pretty close to having a conversation with your friend or neighbor. The biggest difference is that the focus stays on you and doesn't shift to someone else.

Over the years, I have seen my fill of heartache and grief and sadness. I have sat with people knowing full well I couldn't "fix" anything (another common misconception about therapy we will discuss). I was sitting with them, knowing all I could do was hold their hand while they hurt, both figuratively and literally.

So, another reason for writing this book is for laughter. Mixed in with the pain, I have taught people how to laugh, how to see the silly in themselves and those around them. I've demonstrated to others how to look for the silver lining, see the shining sun, and be the ray of sunshine.

All three of my children have worked the front desk for me at some point or another. A couple of years ago, as I finished up a session with someone and walked them out, my daughter Brooke stopped me to ask a question. She asked me why I was laughing with a client that had just left. She commented that she'd heard so much laughter and she didn't know that therapy was funny.

I paused for a moment as I realized, that is probably what most people think. Therapy doesn't have to be all sadness, and crying and frustration. Although that can be good for growth, so can laughter. I explained to her that I teach people how to laugh. We need more laughter in our lives, don't we? I wasn't laughing at my client—I was laughing with her. Teaching her how to see the funny in her own life. Who doesn't feel better after a good belly laugh?

There is a word that I don't use very often. It's the word 'hope'. Hope is a feeling of expectation and desire for a certain thing to happen. It's wishing on a star. I don't believe in hope. I choose to take the actions necessary in order to progress in the way that I want—not just to desire change. However, I hope this book gives you the courage to take the steps needed so that you can make a difference in your life and in the lives around you.

As you turn the pages of this book, I trust you will find inspiration, laughter, and even learning opportunities. Everything in this book was inspired by real people. Rest assured, I have not in any way, provided identifying information. Everyone's confidentiality has been maintained to the highest degree. I have changed gender, age, and enough details to protect those mentioned here.

This book is divided into two main parts. Part one, and the majority of the text, is made of several blogs that I have written over the years. Some were inspired by specific clients I was working with at the time. Others were inspired by being a single mom of three children for many years. The second part of the book is mostly one-liners that were shared with me in therapy; things you don't often expect to hear. In no way am I making fun of, mocking, or criticizing people for what they chose to share. I often find laughter in unexpected places. Therapy is crucial for helping people transform their lives, and I believe laughter is the best modality for doing so.

Chapter 2
Beaten But Not Broken

Several years ago, I was asked to give a keynote presentation in Orlando, Florida. This group was for foster care youth, as well as those working within the field. The group was attended by people on a national level and they met annually all over the country.

To say that point in my life was chaotic would be an understatement. It came as no surprise to me, therefore, that when I arrived at the event, I was slightly overwhelmed and a little confused. I was under the impression I would be presenting to roughly 200 people, which would have been the largest group for me to have spoken to at that time. The actual presentation was attended by over 600 attendees. It was in the grand ballroom of a mega-hotel.

I had prepared a 20-minute presentation, but I actually needed to speak for 45 minutes. So the night before the big event, I was in my hotel room, panic-stricken, and adding material to my talk.

When it was over, I walked off the stage and walked to where my children were sitting. I sat down, still trembling, and asked meekly "How do you think I did?" My oldest daughter, bravely holding back tears, pointed behind me. What seemed like the entire 600-people audience was standing there, waiting to talk to me, hug me, and give me praise.

This was the first time I had shared my personal story in any public forum. It was also the first time my children heard most of what I shared. They were 15, 17, and 20 at the time. And they didn't know.....until that day.

That presentation changed my life, probably more than it did for anyone else in the room, except maybe my kids who were with me. They later shared that they began to see me in a whole new light, and started understanding me more than they could have before.

I am including this in the book because no one cares how much you know until they know how much you care. This is why I care.

Here's what I shared that day:

Thank you _____. It is both an honor and a privilege to be here today and to be part of this program. But, apparently, I didn't pay close enough attention when accepting the invitation. For some reason, I thought there might only be about 200 people in attendance, and well, looks like a whole bunch more of ya'll showed up this morning. Luckily, I brought my own support group with me. I've got Derrick, he's in the back holding up signs that say 'slow down' and 'speed up'. My best friend Lauren is here to make funny faces in case I start to cry. My son Wesley, well he won't be listening to a word that I say, which is pretty typical for him. My girls are also here; Brittany and Brooke; one looks like me and one acts like me, so ya'll see if you can locate them in the crowd!

So, you know how last week, we were all watching the weather and anticipating Hurricane Erika? I'm probably the only person in this room that was hoping that the Hurricane would start in South Florida, and just work her way up all through Florida to prevent me from being here today. But, Erika had other plans, and here I stand before you.

From the moment I accepted the invitation to be one of the keynote speakers, I have been struggling with what to say and how to say it. In my mind, I've played the words over and over, and in the end, I decided this is it. I really am going to publicly, and for the first time, share my personal and difficult story. This is an account of pain, abuse, neglect, and abandonment, and how it shaped my life and ultimately my career choice. At last, I will be able to describe my finding of a personal sense of confidence, fulfillment, professional success, and yes, even love.

This is the first time I've shared most of these stories; not even my children have heard them. So bear with me if I have a momentary pause or crack in my voice, for at times, I am sure a frightened simple girl from Alabama will be staring at you with tear-soaked eyes from behind this podium.

You can't truly appreciate how far I've come without knowing where I started. So, as with all good stories, I'll start at the very beginning and give you the background information! This story has a lot of twists and turns, and ups and downs, and will often sound just like an episode right from Jerry Springer.

I was born in Birmingham, Alabama, and my parents were 41 and 46 at the time of my birth. Both had previously been married; mama had six kids and my dad had three. They got married and had me. This made me the youngest of ten kids. My brothers and sisters were between five and 25 years older than me, and all had moved out except for one brother who was five years older than me, James. James had a stroke not long after I was born, and this paralyzed the entire left side of his body. His development was forever delayed and he was placed in special education programs all throughout school.

So, with this large blended family, of his, hers, and ours, holidays were especially challenging. Christmas was the worst. We celebrated twice each year; having one gathering for mama's kids and a separate get together for my dad's kids. It wasn't until many years later that I came to learn the true reason for the two parties. The two sets of siblings hated each other and together they hated me the most. It would take even longer before I learned the reason for that hatred.

My dad had a remarkable military career, including serving in two wars. At the age of five, we moved from Birmingham to a small town outside of Anniston, Alabama called Eastaboga. It was there that I experienced the first of many episodes of violence at the hand of my dad.

By the time I was nine, I was already a passionate reader. I would read anything that I could get my hands on. I would read billboard signs, magazines, even junk mail. There was never enough time to lose myself in the pages of a good book. Until that one night - you know the night. The one. The one that changes your life forever. The one where your innocence is lost and the harsh cruelty of the world becomes painfully evident. The moment you stop being a child and you are converted to an ever-growing statistic. But this was not something from a book, and it certainly wasn't a fairy tale

It had gotten late and was past my bedtime, so I sought refuge to stay up late and read. I hid out in the bathroom. When I came out into the dark hallway, my dad was waiting for me. With a never before seen anger in his eyes he hurled me back into the bathroom, up against the towel rack, and struck me right across the face. I laid there, not necessarily crying but in shock, staring up at the man who I had ran to for safety and comfort in the past; my protector. But I was now staring into the face of a mad man, with the book still clenched in my hand, the papers ripped in the struggle. Afterwards, he was remorseful for acting so extremely and he apologized profusely. But even then I knew it would happen again.

Like with many patterns of abuse, there are periods of calm between and before the next storm.

In my case, those breaks became shorter and his rage intensified with each new episode. His patterns progressed to extreme over-reacting with severe physical abuse, with me as his only victim. My mother was always close by and would be able to yell at him to snap him out of his trance-like state. Knowing that there was no alcohol or drugs involved, he most likely suffered from extreme Post Traumatic Stress Disorder as a result of his tours of duty. Thankfully, he never once attacked my brother. I don't know why.

I had been the apple of my daddy's eye for my entire life. I could do no wrong in his eyes, and now, all of a sudden, I could do nothing right for him. It affected every area of my life. As you can imagine, I was brokenhearted and bewildered. My grades slipped, I started gaining weight, and I began acting out in school, something that I had never done before. My teachers were asking me what was going on and I told them! I told anyone that would listen that, "My daddy beats me", and yet everyone turned a blind eye. So often kids will not discuss what goes on at home. Here I was begging for someone to help me, and yet it took five years before anyone would listen. It was five long years before someone would step forward and bring this vicious cycle of abuse to an end. (pause)

The next few years took a physical and mental toll on mama. She was never the most positive person to begin with, but having to constantly protect me against my dad's attacks, led to her resenting me more and more. I couldn't understand why she always chose him over me. Her resentment was towards me, and yet he was the adult causing the problems.

I looked for things to be good at, always seeking some sort of adult approval. I started cross-stitching, and spent many hours alone, making beautiful works of art that I would frame and give away to my siblings, friends, neighbors; anyone that might repay me with just a kind word. One night, after completing a project, I cut the fabric too small for the intended frame and took it to mama for her to somehow fix it. I was crying and said in frustration, "I just can't do anything right", hoping to finally hear a word of encouragement. She responded by agreeing with me and taking that opportunity to once again tell me that I would never be good at anything.

Another instance, probably around the same time; we were out shopping and we were putting some things in the car. Mama slammed the trunk down on my hand. In my tears of pain, I said to her, its okay, I know you didn't mean to. I will never forget her anger and rage as she said to me that it was my fault for having my hand in the way in the first place. Never a kind word, and never a single word of encouragement from her.

My dad soon retired, and we moved to the nearby Talladega, Alabama so that we would be closer to his favorite golf course. Both mama and my brother were convinced this was just the change needed that would fix all of our problems. Unfortunately, we all knew the truth, and that his inner demons would not be eliminated with a change of scenery, or the recreational activity of playing golf.

Another good reason to make the move to Talladega was that two of my sisters on my mother's side lived there. They were affiliated with the Alabama School for the Deaf and Blind, both of them having been born legally blind. Eventually, I learned the reason for their disability. It was the direct result of my mother taking an abortion pill that didn't quite work either time. Rather, it resulted in their loss of vision, along with other health issues.

Changing gears, let me tell you about probably the only thing that our family could agree on, that was good ole fashioned home cooking. We didn't eat out much, because mama cooked everything from scratch, and she was a great cook. That is probably the only positive thing you'll ever hear me say about her. And being from the south, we did not eat POTATOES, we ate Taters. Every Sunday morning and only on Sunday mornings, Mama cooked fried taters and biscuits for us.

Shortly after our move to Talladega, I'm walking towards the kitchen as she's cooking the taters. I'm sure you have gathered by now; we were not a church-going family, and we did not use words like "blessing". And let me also say this….even as a young teenager, I have always been a nosey girl. I love a good story, I love to eavesdrop, and I love to hear gossip. I would never repeat gossip, of course, I only listen... Anyway, I'm walking towards the kitchen, and I overhear my parents talking. I hear mama tell my dad that, "it would be a blessing" to get rid of me. I was 13 years old.

From that moment on, I lived in constant fear of how and when they may get rid of me. After all, my mother had taken a medication to try and abort at least one of my sisters, and I had just found out about that. I began to sleep with a light on in my room. My dad told me repeatedly not to leave the light on, but I was certain that if I turned it off just once something terrible would happen to me. One night, as I slept, my dad came into my room and took the lamp from my nightstand. He took it to his woodshop and chopped into tiny pieces with his ax. He returned all the pieces to my room and put it back on my nightstand. He told me the next day that if I ever disobeyed him again, I would be the next thing that he chopped with his ax. I knew at that moment, if I was ever going to be safe, I would have to leave.

Fast forward a few months to my 14th birthday, and my brother and I go to the local skating rink. On our way home, we give a friend a ride home causing us to be late by about 20 minutes. My dad was waiting up for us. He immediately began yelling. By now, this is an all too familiar full-on rage. Backing me into a corner as soon as I walk in the front door, with his hands around my throat, he began to choke me. I had learned to fight him off of me by going for his man-parts, but this time, I was losing consciousness. Mama walked up behind him to stop him, he stepped backwards and broke her foot, truly by accident, or so he claimed. That was the last time she ever intervened on my behalf. Even after that incident, it took three months before I was placed in an emergency shelter while a more suitable placement could be located.

To this day, I struggle with having Happy Birthday sang to me.

I'm not really sure exactly what led to the Department of Children and Family Services becoming involved. But I think it might have had something to do with my dad constantly calling the police to tell them that I was an unruly teenager that wasn't listening. He wanted them to arrest me. And each time the police would come out, they would ask what I was doing wrong. Well, I wasn't sneaking out, I wasn't doing drugs, I wasn't breaking any laws, and the police soon realized that I wasn't the problem.

When it came time to go to the emergency shelter, three months after the incident on my 14th birthday, it was midsummer, and I was allowed to pack only a few things. I was picked up by two social workers and driven half an hour away to the shelter. It was the first time that I can ever remember being hugged by mama. My dad was out golfing when I left.

After my 30 days in the shelter, it was decided that I would live with my sister and her husband, who also lived in our neighborhood. Interesting twist here; my sister had two children younger than me that she wasn't raising, and who she had walked away from after her divorce a few years prior. In fact, she didn't even visit with her children, and they lived in another state. But, somehow, the state of Alabama thought she was fit to raise me? I stayed with her for two months before I packed my bags and moved back home. My sister was 14 years older than me, and she was on her second marriage. It bothered her that I was home in the afternoons with her husband, when he got home from work before her. He and I got along fine, and it was never weird or inappropriate for me and him, only her. Oh, and she had roaches. I couldn't do the roaches.

Even though it was a small house, everywhere I went I carried a can of Raid with me, ready to fend off these pesky little creatures. One night I come back from the bathroom, and I flip on the light, as I look down at my pillow. There he is. The grossest, biggest, creepiest roach crawling across my pillow. I went home the next day.

I was home with my parents for nearly six months before my social worker knew I had moved.

So, I'm back home, and things were quiet and somewhat normal for a short while. You know, that honeymoon period? But Einstein said it best when he defined insanity as doing the same thing over and over again and expecting different results. One night my dad overheard me on the phone. Somehow, he misinterpreted the conversation, and not bothering to ask questions, he thought I was trying to make plans to leave the house. He came up behind me and slammed me down onto the couch and we eventually ended up on the floor. There he took a decorative basket of pinecones and proceeded to slam my face again and again into their sharp edges, leaving my cheeks indented with their profile for the next several days.

After my social worker learned of the pinecone incident, it was decided that something else had to be done. Apparently, my dad underwent an evaluation by the VA. Remember, he wasn't a drinker. I remember my parents telling me that the decision had to be made that either he or I had to leave the house permanently. Well, in my mind, since I wasn't the one causing the problem, clearly it would be him that had to go. Silly me, I was wrong!

One summer morning, the phone kept ringing, and I finally woke up to answer it. It was my social worker. She was calling to tell me that she had a placement for me at a group foster home three hours away, and I would be leaving in a few days. I remember thinking it was odd that she never asked to speak to mama to give her any of the details. She just gave me all of the information and we hung up. Ironically, when I finally found my mama to tell her about the phone call, she was outside picking up pinecones to replace the ones that had been ruined in the recent scuffle. Imagine my surprise when I learned that she already knew that I was leaving, she just didn't have the courage to tell me. I guess she finally got the blessing she was hoping for.

Mama went with the social worker to take me to the girl's ranch on a Sunday in August, not long before school started that year. They dropped me off at a house with eight other girls and a set of house parents that clearly I'd never met before. There were no tears shed by anyone when the social worker and mama drove away. I spent the first hour or so unpacking, and then I sat alone in that big empty bedroom. I didn't know anyone, and the other girls were doing their own things, so they didn't bother with me. Sadly, I had no books to read, so I sat and stared out the window for hours until dinner time.

When school started a few days later, I had to fill out all of that new student paperwork. I didn't even know the names of the house parents, the address where I lived, or a phone number to put down. I remember walking up to the teacher in front of the entire class to say that I didn't know what to write on the forms. She said very loudly, deliberately trying to embarrass me, "You don't know your parents' names?" before realizing where I lived. 25 years later, I can still remember what that teacher looked like.

I spent the school year at the Alabama Sheriff's Girls Ranch. I went to the dentist for the first time, EVER. I had at least one cavity in every single tooth. You see, not only did my parents abuse me physically, emotionally, and verbally, they also neglected me. I had never been to the doctor or the dentist.

This wasn't for a lack of health care, or a lack of transportation. Mama was a stay at home mom. She didn't have to schedule appointments around her work schedule. She just didn't take the time to take care of me.

Okay, stay with me, here, it's gonna get tricky. During my year at the Girls Ranch, my dad found out that my mother's ex-husband had also moved to Talladega. He moved there to also be near the kids that he and my mother shared. My dad was beyond furious. My dad divorced my mother and moved back to Birmingham. He started writing me letters, and he was so sweet and so kind, so very sorry for all of the wrongdoing. I think he had started getting some counseling, and was probably on some medication. My dad revealed something to me that he and my mother had been very ashamed of. They were not married when she became pregnant with me. Now, of course, in today's world, that's not a big deal at all, but back in the early '70s, that was a really big deal, and my dad was very remorseful.

As a result of their divorce, I was discharged from the ranch at the end of that school year and I returned to live with mama. Despite their divorce, my parents continued to see one another. And once again, I found myself thrust back into the abusive cycle, and the gentle giant that my dad had turned into during their divorce was gone. By this time, I'm 15, and I was forced to be with them every minute.

One Friday night, my dad arrived at the house and wanted us to go with him to his house about an hour away. I refused, and I can even remember saying this is against my case plan. I could hear him telling mama that he had a way to make me go with him. We both knew that he had recently purchased a gun, which he kept under the driver's seat of his car. He went to the car to get his gun. This was it. It was finally happening; I was going to die this night. He was going to shoot me. Initially, I was immobilized with fear, and just like in the movies, things were in slow motion. As I heard the car door slam, with the understanding that he was headed back inside, I jumped into action. I grabbed two things; my contact case and contact solution, and jumped out my bedroom window. I hitched a ride across town to my other sister's house. I hid out there all weekend. My sister covered for me, and Monday morning I called my social worker. She called the Girls Ranch and got me back in, and I stayed there until I graduated from high school two years later.

My mother never ever, in her whole life, said a kind thing to me. She often told me that I was fat; she told me that I was ugly. She loved telling me that I would never find a man that would love me. Even though she never took me to the dentist, she told me that my teeth were ugly, and that was just another reason that no one would ever love me. She reminded me every day that none of my siblings liked me. As much as she claimed that she hated me and my dad fighting, she actually instigated most of the arguments between us.

Despite all of her actions and her lack of actions towards me, she actually had the audacity to feel betrayed by me, because I chose living at the Girls Ranch over living with her. For months, she would write letters to me about how disloyal I was to her and how much I had let her down. I held my ground and stayed at my refuge as long as I possibly could. Eventually, her anger gave way and we visited every so often on the weekends, and on the holidays. For many years in a row, my parents would drive three hours to pick me up, and we'd drive three hours back to their house. The only place open was a gas station a small town. This gas station had a deli style-selection of various fried foods and two booths. It wasn't much, but there was no fighting, and it was our Christmas dinner.

Upon my parents' reconciliation, my dad gave Mama an ultimatum. They would remarry only if she would agree to never see her children again. Not only did she agree to this, she told everyone that he had made her agree to this. As you can imagine, this caused great animosity in an already chaotic family situation.

After graduation, the Girls Ranch set me up in a dorm room so I could start college. I lived about 20 minutes away from my parents, and that worked out well. I was close enough to them to get along, yet they were not responsible for me in any way, so there were no stressors. I still desperately wanted my parents' approval and unconditional love. I was so empty and lonely on the inside, still playing those recordings over and over in my head; you're fat, you're ugly, and you'll never find a man to love you. Even though the relationship was okay now, there was nothing positive being said, but I kept hanging around hoping to hear it anyway. After all, they bought me a car for graduation, which must mean they liked me, right?

One night, through mutual friends, I met a young man home on leave from the Navy. After a few weekend meetings, I married him and moved to California. He was the first guy that told me that I was pretty, and he seemed to mean it, so that must be love. Ten years and three children later, I realized that as wonderful as he was, it wasn't love, and we didn't belong together. So, I gathered up a whole lot of courage, my three kids, and got a divorce. He and I remain close friends today.

After a mother that resented me, and a dad that suffered with mental illness, nine siblings that hated me for no apparent reason, and marrying the first guy that came along, I always knew there had to be more to life. Instinctively, I knew somehow, someway, there was some other reason that I was put here on this Earth. I had a purpose, and I had to find it. And then it happened. I became a mom. Despite the fancy degrees, and overcoming a childhood of pain and adversity, being a mom is without a doubt my greatest achievement. Of course, the only thing that I could learn from my own mama was what NOT to do. And I hate admitting that I've made way too many mistakes with my children. I can only hope that, as they become parents many many many years from now, they will have had a better role model than I did.

One Thanksgiving, I was visiting my parents, with my three children, while their dad was out to sea, serving on a United States nuclear submarine. The kids at the time were five, two, and six years. During dinner my oldest, Brittany made a comment about how her skirt was too tight, and I clearly remember that it was a 6x, a very appropriate size for a five-year-old. Mama commented that she had noticed that Brittany was getting fat. Fat! That was the word she used. A word that I was all too familiar with, as she had used it to describe me for so many years.

Within minutes, I had all three kids loaded up in the car and we were driving away, our Thanksgiving dinner still on the table. I did something that night that I had never been able to do for myself. I protected my own little girl from the harsh cruel words of a bitter old woman.

Some people search for a career path, and others take aptitude tests to learn which field best suits them. Because a foster care placement saved my life, I always knew that I had to become the change that I wanted to see. While being a Navy wife, moving often, and having three pregnancies, I still managed to get a Bachelor's Degree from Auburn, and a Master's Degree from Florida State, both in Social Work. I'm halfway through completing my PhD in Clinical Psychology. I have over 16 years of experience in working with individuals, couples, and families. I've been a Licensed Clinical Social Worker in Florida since 2009. For four years, I taught psychology courses at the University of Phoenix. I've conducted over 75 parenting plans, and I've written 100 comprehensive child and family assessments for children placed in foster care. I've been court-appointed to provide individual, group, and family counseling. Next week, I'll be completing my Certification in Death and Grief Studies through Colorado State University. And, I'm thrilled and honored that my daughter Brooke will be with me, taking her first class as I complete that program.

In 2008, I ventured out and founded a nonprofit adoption agency, first in Georgia and then expanded to Florida. I was never in a situation to be adopted, but I wanted to help create as many happy and healthy families as possible. Last year, after six years and just over 40 private adoptions, I handed over the reins and stepped down as Executive Director. Running simultaneously with the adoption agency, I also started a private practice. I now have two offices, with a psychiatrist, a nurse-practitioner, and five therapists. We see about 100 patients a week.

You've heard me say that foster care saved my life. Even after raising three teenagers as a single mom, I have never been arrested, and I don't smoke, drink, or do drugs. Let me tell you about my siblings and how they are doing today.

I'm from Alabama, we don't have a family tree, we have a wreath, and it just goes in circles. My oldest brother is 66, and he's currently in prison for getting his 16-year old daughter pregnant several years ago. Two sets of nieces and nephews have children together. Another brother served a 15-year sentence for DUI manslaughter. The two oldest brothers fathered 14 children that we know of. All of my siblings have been in jail or prison. All of them smoke cigarettes, marijuana, or dip tobacco. All of them are, or have been, more than just social drinkers. None of them graduated from college, and only two of them graduated from high school. Five are on some type of disability, two have died, and one estranged herself from the family 20 years ago. Only one has any teeth.

Aside from career victories and the success of being a mom to my three treasures, there is another great ending to my story. Not long after I had my first child, my dad found an inner peace within himself. I'm sure that some type of medication played a major role in helping him find that peace, but nevertheless, he found it. My children adored him and had the greatest relationship with him. It was such a joy watching him love and spoil them. He and I were able to make amends, and I forgave him, for everything. When he died, nothing else needed to be said, and all was forgiven and forgotten. There were over 300 people at his funeral. He was truly an honorable man, with many hidden demons that he was able to overcome. I am so proud to be his daughter. He's been gone for 12 years now. My children have happy memories of him and, until today, didn't really know this other side of him.

As for mama, she remained bitter until the very end. She was diagnosed with lung cancer a year before she died. Being the good daughter, and still desperate for her unconditional love and acceptance, I brought her into my home and cared for her during chemotherapy and radiation treatments while raising three small children. She was so ungrateful, and as mean as always. After two months, I put her on a plane and sent her home. As I walked up to her casket at the funeral, the song from the Wizard of Oz played in my head, Ding Dong, the Witch is Dead. It took me until I was 33 years old to learn that she would never love and accept me, but it wasn't because there was something wrong with me, there was something wrong with her.

And three years ago, I finally learned the biggest secret that my family had been keeping. My half-sister on my mother's side died at the young age of 53 from a sudden heart attack. I was given the high honor of speaking at her funeral, a moment that I will always treasure, as she's the one that hid me in her bedroom closet the weekend that I ran for safety from a mad-man with a gun. After the funeral, I went to visit my half-sister on my dad's side at her home. I finally learned the truth. You see, my dad's first wife was dying of cancer. She would be at home, with her terminal illness, and her teenage children. My mother was married to an alcoholic. She would deliberately provide him with enough alcohol to get him drunk to where he'd pass out. Then my parents would meet up somewhere. This ultimately led to the pregnancy of me. I'm the product of my parents' affair. It all finally clicked!

The separate Christmas parties, the bitterness towards me, the reason the two sides couldn't be in the same room, the lie about my parents' original wedding date…….

I've spent most of my life in a struggle with self-hatred, desperately hoping that one day I could be good enough, pretty enough, thin enough, smart enough, something enough. It's only been in the last few years that I've realized that I don't have to struggle anymore. That struggle is over. I won.

As I look out over this podium, I see so many individuals, each, I am certain, with their own unique story to tell. I imagine many are similar to mine, and some even worse, with a hurt and desolation that few of us would dare even imagine. But I say with full-throated confidence that if we as individuals are to overcome our tortured past we must remain resolute in our own self-worth and find a common inner strength and continue to fight the daily struggle that is life.

We must also accept that at times our difficulties will surpass our own physical, mental, or emotional abilities. It is at times such as these that we must recognize our own vulnerabilities, and seek and accept assistance from others. To put it simply; you can't always do it by yourself.

There is a deficiency in foster care services and quality mental health care. We must challenge others within our community, state, and local government to rise to the ever-increasing need for improved resources. We must embark on a mission to make services more accessible, and to minimize the negative stigma placed on today's fractured foster care mental health industry.

My personal belief is that the blessing my mother had hoped for so early on in my life is now mine to fulfill, but in a much different way than she imagined. I was a burden to my parents, but I no longer live in fear and I will not remain their victim. And I'm much more than a survivor of child abuse. I have, and I will continue to, hold fast and live, cherishing every day that I have. I surround myself with people that I love and that love me. With these principles, I have overcome my past and will continue to fulfill my time on this Earth attempting to help others find their own path through the forest of trials and tribulations.

In closing, I'd like to share with you the words of Maya Angelou, "People will forget what you said, people will forget what you did, but people will never forget how you made them feel."

Thank you.

Chapter 3
10 Reasons to Talk to a Therapist

When life pulls the rug out from under us, therapy can help. Maybe you've considered talking to someone. Yet, maybe, your fears of what it will be like are preventing you from getting the help you need. Why should you consider talking to a therapist? As I shared in Chapter 1, the majority of people who do choose to seek help reported feeling better. And I know you want to feel better.

Keep this in mind though. When people go see a band and they don't like it — they never go see that particular band again. They will go to see other bands and enjoy them immensely, and they probably have a favorite band. For some reason, people don't see therapists like that. We all get lumped together. If you see a bad therapist, you think all therapists are bad. Little secret — we're not. You'll find one that you mesh well with, just as long as you don't give up if you are unlucky enough to meet the bad one first.

1. Change happens; therapy provides a companion for the journey.

Sometimes things happen that we're not comfortable discussing with our friends or family. A therapist is an impartial listener who provides a safe sounding board, someone to look at the pros and cons of possible choices. Most of the time, we need to talk to someone to help us get some perspective on life events.

2. Therapy improves your mental health.

For many people, anxiety and/or depression is a recurrent experience. Talk therapy has been shown to be helpful in working through anxiety and depression_by providing support for the discussion of underlying issues that may be contributing to the anxiety and depression, as well as teaching skills to help lessen the side-effects.

3. Therapy improves your ability to regain balance faster after a life-altering event that causes grief and loss.

Grief and loss are parts of life, whether it's the loss of a job, pet, relationship, or physical ability. Therapy is a way to work through the grief process with support.

4. A therapist is an impartial person to talk to about negative emotions/thoughts/etc. that surround caregiving, such as with a new infant, elderly parent, or spouse.

Taking care of a loved one can be difficult, especially over a long period of time. As caregivers, we are human, and we can sometimes experience feelings of frustration and anger as we become tired and overwhelmed. Talking to a therapist about any negative thoughts or feelings can provide a place to release and normalize these feelings, and help you to be able to return to your caregiving role.

5. Therapists can provide perspective, normalizing events in our lives.

Most people, at some point in their lives, wonder if the thoughts, feelings, and behaviors they are experiencing are normal. Because of the wide variety of people and situations that therapists have encountered, they can provide a sense of perspective about your experience. If there is some concern about what is happening, a therapist can support you as you move in the right direction.

6. Therapy provides an opportunity to heal from past trauma.

Everyone has "baggage"; past events in their lives that affect how they cope in the present. We often think of trauma as big things — the sudden death of a loved one, a car accident, an assault — but trauma is extremely personal and could be something that may appear to be small to some people, while it can be a major stumbling block for others. A therapist can help you to cope with and/or move beyond your trauma, so you can see positive changes in your life.

7. Therapy is your first recourse when a key person in your life is concerned about you and suggests that you "talk to someone."

It is sometimes the people that are closest to us that can best see when we need help. Often, we become so used to our negative coping strategies that we don't notice them anymore. If a key person in your life is telling you of their concerns, please listen and think about what they are saying. Getting help may make all the difference to taking control of your life.

8. Therapy can help when you are suffering from bodily symptoms that are not helped with physical treatments, such as stomach aches, headaches, and muscle tension.

Our bodies are amazing things. Sometimes they tell us what our minds are choosing to ignore. The body holds on to negative emotions and past trauma. When physical treatments are not working, it may be time to look elsewhere for both the cause and the treatment.

9. Therapy can help when you are self-soothing using inappropriate methods, such as drugs, alcohol, and over-spending.

Most of us will resort to "comfort" food after a bad day at work or an argument with a friend. However, when we are doing this daily, or if our self-soothing behavior has moved on to activities that hurt rather than help, it's time to get help.

10. Therapy can help when an important relationship is going through a rough patch, or falling apart.

Relationships are tricky things. They require work, and sometimes they get off-track. Seeing a therapist can provide tools and a forum to help get a relationship past the rough patch, as well as providing support if a relationship is ending.

These are just ten reasons to see a therapist; there are as many reasons as there are individuals, couples, and families. Everyone who comes to counseling does so with their own story and situation. If you see yourself in any of these reasons, seeing a therapist may be the next step. The best part is, even if you decide it's not the right fit for you — chances are you are still better off than when you began.

Chapter 4
Thoughts About Motherhood

Being a child of abuse brings about enormous lifelong effects that are never fully understood by those around us. The type of abuse doesn't necessarily make a difference. All children of abuse face lifelong battles.

Being someone who was physically abused, neglected, and emotionally destroyed as a child and adolescent, doesn't make me a victim. I don't consider myself a victim, but rather a survivor of child abuse. All along the way, I could sense God's presence, despite the difficulties of my childhood. I was eventually removed three times before I didn't have to go back anymore. I was placed into a group foster home, run by wonderful people, who provided unconditional love, and taught Christian morals and values.

As an adult, I married and started having children. Somewhere along the way, my relationship with my dad, the primary perpetrator was restored. We were able to mend, and he sought out my true forgiveness, which I easily gave. The relationship with my mother was not so easily fixed.

My mother was born in 1932, along with her twin. Born to poor farmers at the onset of the Great Depression, one day she and all of her siblings were just given away. Well before adoption was legalized, she and the siblings were handed over to various people in their community, in pairs of two.

My mother and her twin were raised together, and they eventually reunited with their other siblings as adults. Mother married at 15, and had her first child at 16. Unfortunately, she married an alcoholic, who also had the physical disability of having only one leg. The two would remain together for over 20 years, having 5 more children together.

Even prior to their divorce, she was having an affair with my dad. My dad was not the least bit innocent here. His wife was dying of cancer while he was out and about with my mother. Their union resulted in a pregnancy with her 7th child, his 4th child, at ages 41 and 46 respectively.

My dad was a war veteran, having served in both World War II and the Korean War. He was very dedicated to serving this country, and spent 44 years enlisted and in the reserves. However, as you can imagine, his mental health was questionable, after years of military service and his own unfortunate childhood. He was born to Italian immigrants, who could not read or write. His mother died early and his father remarried, and had between 7 and 9 children altogether. His stepmother was abusive, and refused to allow all of the kids to eat, have clothes, or be treated equally.

When someone is abused, they often fear rejection. It wasn't until I became an adult that I could actually name this process for what it was. All through childhood, my automatic thoughts were, "that person won't like me", "there's no way that person will want to be my friend".

Healing takes time. It's harder than we think and if truth be known, you can't really do it alone. God, friends, family, and a good support system are practically a requirement.

As a bereavement counselor, I work with many people who have lost a child. Having a child die before you do goes against the rules we all know naturally. The old die first, the young live to be old before they die. Whether it is a homicide or some type of terminal illness, having to say goodbye to a child is devastating. The age of that child doesn't make a difference to a parent's grief. Whether the child is 5, 25, or 45, they are still someone's child.

Grief comes in many forms, and any loss can be devastating. Divorce, job loss, infertility, or moving can all be issues that cause us to grieve. Many times, those issues are things that we have no control over. The economy downsizes, we lose our job and have to move. Doctors can't always explain or reverse infertility. Our spouse of many years leaves us for a newer, younger, version.

When a death occurs, especially a sudden death, no one has an opportunity to say goodbye. There is often unfinished business left forever undone. As a mother grieves, everyone around her feels a sense of the loss being experienced. There is sadness, and yet well-meaning people don't know what to say.

Yet, we all lose our children one way or another. Who was it that decided that at age 18, parents go from supervisor to spectator? Real grownups know that at 18, knowledge is limited and arrogance is plentiful. Our children are desperate for independence, and yet too immature to realize its gravity, yet we must allow apron strings to be cut; kicking, fighting, and screaming maybe, but we have no choice.

Years ago, I had the unfortunate experience of grieving for what seemed to be the worst situation. Yes, having to bury your child is devastating. Losing your job and having to move is overwhelming. Not being able to have a biological child is crushing. What about this? Having a child turn 18 and decide you are not her mother anymore? There is no way to "announce" this to others, without the fear of their judgment against you. There is no listing in the newspaper, no legal papers to file, no other methods to attempt to repair the situation.

Unfortunately, it happened to me. Shortly after my daughter turned 18, she decided she was an adult and didn't have to follow the rules anymore. Her father and I spoke with her countless times about her behavior, attitude, and overall outlook. Her response….."I'm an adult now".

We've all seen the popular photo on social media that says, "Teenagers: Tired of being harassed by your stupid parents? Act Now! Move out, get a job, pay your own bills, do it now while you still know everything". Now, we think in the real world this can't just happen. The teenager has to have some way to live and have a roof over their head.

Regrettably, in my situation, my daughter found a family to buy into her sad story of not getting along with me. Of course, it was a one-sided story, filled with teenage understanding, or lack thereof. This family decided to welcome my daughter with open arms. This was despite my attempts to speak with the family, and try to give them an adult perspective of the situation.

In the first two months of my daughter living with her new family, she missed numerous days of school, was in danger of not graduating, went to an out of town concert, and got a relatively large tattoo. The family even requested "child support", and implied that they would like to claim her on their taxes.

When a child chooses to walk out of your life, with no explanation, there is no opportunity to say goodbye.

There is unfinished business, with an uncertainty of what that unfinished business might be. No one knows exactly what to say, and there is the constant fear of judgment. "What kind of mother lets this happen?" "Look at how badly she screwed up, her own child doesn't want to live with her."

Do I take it personally? You're damned right I do. All my life, I've feared the rejection of others. My mother chose a man over me, and she made it known to anyone who would listen. So I thought, when I had children, I would be such a different kind of mom they would never reject me. Life has a funny way of showing you things you didn't expect to see.

How did this happen, you might be asking? And why am I writing about it? I'm not sure I can answer the former, but I have a few answers for the latter.

How did this happen? I have no idea. I'm a therapist, a social worker, an adoption specialist. I have been a do-gooder and a good-doer. I have spent the last 15 years putting families together, helping bring about resolutions, and walking with those as they create their happily ever after. How did I miss the mark on my own daughter? I wish I had an easy answer.

How did I get replaced so easily? I was a stay at home mom for the first 8 years of my daughter's life. We are inseparable, two peas in a pod. She's the "spitting image" of me, I've heard others say. Poof, now she's gone. And the pain is unbearable. I'm not getting the chance to enjoy her senior year, shop for a prom dress, or pick out graduation invitations. I rarely hear from her, and I struggle to continue saying that I have an 18-year old daughter. In her mind, she has a new mom now.

Why am I writing about this? Why am I airing my own dirty laundry? Those are easier questions to answer. No one is a perfect parent. Sometimes you do everything you know to do, and it still doesn't work out the way you had hoped it would. Attorneys get divorced, policemen get arrested, and accountants go bankrupt. And, yes, sometimes, therapists have to say goodbye to their own child, realizing that somewhere along the way, something went wrong. Undiagnosed mental illness? Poor parenting? Teenage crap? A good-for-nothing, meddling family? Assigning blame never really helps anything.

I move forward each day, smiling and continuing to help others. Another sign I read today, "Happiness is not a destination, but rather a way of life". You can't argue with that.

Update: Brittany and I eventually turned a corner and things improved for us. It took years. I had to apologize for something I didn't know I'd done (and still don't). I also accepted an apology that I never actually received. Maybe all is forgiven, but it's never forgotten. For her as well I would imagine.

Chapter 5
What Are The Rules?

Back when my middle daughter was 11, she brought home a list of rules offered to her by her best friend. Now, I have no idea where these rules originated, and if memory serves me correctly, I've probably seen these rules as a forwarded email at least once or twice. But as I read them, I realized I really like most of them, and I wished that all parents would agree and adopt these rules.

Rule #1 states "Life is not fair—get used to it".

Back when my children were younger, I always wanted to be fair. If one child received something, I felt it was my duty to ensure an equal division among the others. If one child was having a birthday party, then surely I must get them all a present. Please tell me you've been there too. And no, I am not a socialist.

As I've grown and learned through the years, I have realized there are times when no matter what you do, it just ain't gonna be fair. I can't make sure that all of my kids get equal treatment from life at all times, and I can't run myself ragged trying to!

Then what do I say when I get the foot stomp, eye roll, arms crossed and yes, even tears to go along with, "That's not fair". After all, I am a family therapist — I should have some meaningful way of explaining the universe to small children. I've been trained to communicate effectively with others, I can definitely handle this.

Oftentimes, I would try to explain the rationale behind whatever was causing the unequal distribution of goods and/or services. Without hesitation, a child will listen to reason, right? Obviously, I had a lot to learn about being a parent.

As my children have reached preteen and teenage status, I have learned that rule #1 is actually applicable in everyday life. My response to them has also changed drastically. No longer do I attempt to use logic, explanations, and reasoning for any perceptions of unfairness. I have a standard answer to the complaint of, "that's not fair".

My children probably can recite this by memory. I say to them, "you're right, that's not fair, but my job as a parent is to prepare you for the real world, and I'm just doing my job". Wow, isn't that easier — at least on me anyway.

I have decided that I *really* like Rule #1.

Rule #2 is this: "The world won't care about your self-esteem. The world will expect you to accomplish something before you feel good about yourself".

I went through my own adolescence thinking that no one else in the entire world had thoughts and feelings anywhere near similar to mine. Imagine my surprise when I realized that most people do feel similar to the way I do. I was even more surprised when I learned people have insecurities, fears, and worries just like I do. All this time, I thought people were staring at me like I had a third head. When, in reality, they felt like they were the ones with the third head.

In an online support group, a lady shared that she was too uncomfortable to go to the gym because of all of the other people there. She was worried that others would stare at her, for not being in shape. Someone else reminded her that at the gym people are only looking at themselves — not others.

So I tested this theory. The next time I went to the gym, I looked around. The overwhelming majority of men were looking at themselves in the mirror, while the ladies were avoiding the mirror at all costs. How did it become this way? We teach men they are unstoppable but we teach women to hide in the background.

Rule #3: "You will not make $60,000 a year right out of high school. You won't be a vice president with a car phone until you earn both".

I can definitely agree with the first part of this rule. A high school diploma is only a stepping stone. In order to get an advanced career, it will most likely require a four-year-degree and maybe even a graduate degree. Obviously, there are some exceptions, but they are just that......exceptions.

With the current economic crisis, jobs are scarce, and more people are applying for those fewer jobs. Because the potential applicant pool is large, employers can usually get away with paying less and providing fewer benefits. After all, if you won't do the job for what is being offered, there are many more resumes to choose from.

The few high school graduates I know have turned their noses up at entry-level positions in the hopes of a higher position with better pay. Working at a fast-food restaurant right out of high school is not being underemployed; it's a rung up on the ladder. Granted, it may be on a low level, but it's a start.

The second part of this rule probably doesn't apply much anymore. What teenager do you know that doesn't have a cell phone? And, yes, I know that even preteens have them now. When my kids were teenagers, they had friends that had all of the latest and greatest cell phones. I still don't understand how or why parents choose to indulge their children to this extent. Having a phone for communication and convenience is one thing, but a child with a fancy phone and a data package for checking emails….please don't fall into that category of parents.

My kids had a basic boring flip phone, as well as limits on the minutes and text usage. Overages of either result in consequences. Any time they lost the phone privileges, it was painful for them without a doubt.

Rule #4 is this: "If you think your teacher is tough, wait until you get a boss".

This is one of my most favorite rules. School systems vary from place to place, and in my rural community, our teachers and administrators are some of the best. However, we do have those teachers that allow students to go an entire nine-week grading period without completing any assignments. Just before grades are due, the teacher allows the students to complete and submit all assignments. No penalties, no consequences, and the student gets an "A".

Adults know that is not indicative of the real world. If your supervisor asks for a report, chances are they will not intend to be waiting for nine weeks. If that is the case, then consequences such as disciplinary action or termination will surely occur.

I speak from experience. When my middle daughter was in 8th grade, she brought home a progress report and a list of missing assignments that were causing her less than favorable grade in a particular class. Over one weekend, Teacher Mom insisted that all assignments get completed. She turned them in on Monday and her "barely C" went to an "A"...the teacher sent a note home telling me how proud she was of my daughter's efforts.

My daughter thought all was well, but I was not as easy to please as her teacher was. Together we went through her planner of upcoming assignments and scheduled time to ensure completion of each of them prior to the due date. My daughter still thinks I was overreacting. I think the teacher should have higher standards, and insist that due dates be honored.

I have previously had contract and part-time positions for a number of other agencies. I can assure you that if the Executive Director needs something from me, she calls or emails me and expects an immediate response, whether it's my assigned day or not.

Teachers should be helping parents by preparing students for the real world, where deadlines are adhered to, and extra time is not a given, but rather the exception for true emergencies.

Rule #5: "Flipping burgers is not beneath your dignity. Your grandparents had a different word for burger flipping: they called it opportunity."

Somewhere along the way, we have forgotten to teach a work-ethic to our children. There are some adults who never quite picked it up either. Having a full-time mental health practice, with anywhere from 2-20 independent contractors on board at any given time, I've seen this first hand. The hardest position to keep filled is the front office position.

I would estimate that I've had 30 people in that position in the last 11 years. It always goes the same way — they start out doing well, showing energy and positivity. Then there is a shift. They start to think they know more, can do more, or just want things done their way. As a business owner, I'm open to new ideas and strategies; however since I've been doing this a long time, I know how I want it done. So, yeah, just do it my way please.

Working with individuals who are not at their best mentally is a challenge. Mental health is vital to overall health. The first line of contact is the person answering the phone. I could give a list of grievances here over the challenges of teaching people how to work the front desk, but for my own mental health, I'm going to tuck that list away and move on.

Rule #6: "If you mess up, it's not your parent's fault, so don't whine about your mistakes, learn from them."

Growing up in the land of dysfunction, I learned to blame myself for everything. Through the years, after a great deal of therapy, introspection, and self-examination, I began to recognize that my abnormal childhood was definitely not my fault. So I spent a few years blaming my parents for everything in my life. I gave them no credit for anything good (because let's face it, that list was pretty short).

It wasn't until I was a mom of teenagers that I realized no matter how much good you do, some people just aren't going to accept it. Whatever their reason is. People are not always good people. I couldn't let that stop me from doing the right thing though.

Along the way, I have made mistakes that I could learn from. In fact, I'm still making mistakes that I learn from. Most recently, I hired a young girl for the front desk. I knew at the interview she was not the right fit for us. She'd been fired from her two previous positions. Now she hadn't come right out and said this, but it was easy enough to decipher from her descriptions of why she had left her last two places of employment.

I hired her. I wasn't in the best place to be picky, aka I was desperate to get the phones covered. In less than five months, she made more mistakes than I could count, questioned my every move, and ultimately decided to quit without notice, after having a tantrum and running out.

Rule #7: "Before you were born, your parents weren't as boring as they are now. They got that way from paying your bills, cleaning your clothes, and listening to you talk about how cool you thought you were."

As we get older, 9:00 PM becomes the new midnight. I can remember staying up half the night and functioning the next day as normal. Now, I'm in bed almost as the sun goes down (I'm in Florida, so it gets dark late).

I can remember my children at some point or another, saying they couldn't wait to grow up, become adults, and make their own choices. Now, each of them have realized it's a trap. Their own choices equate to paying bills, being responsible, and losing their carefree childhood days. It's a dirty secret and none of us recognize it until it's too late. We become adults and want desperately to go back to naps, the playground, and watching cartoons.

Rule # 8: "Your school may have done away with winners and losers but life has not. In some schools, they have abolished failing grades and they'll give you as many times as you want to get the right answer. This doesn't bear the slightest resemblance to anything in real life."

I used to think school prepared us for real life. Maybe it even used to. Most of the time, however, it's a fantasy land that prepares us falsely for real life. My daughter, in the 8th grade, was given a chance to make up 36 missed assignments so she didn't fail. I can't imagine an employer, a neighbor, a co-worker, or a family member giving you 36 times to do what is expected of you.

Rule #9: "Life is not divided into semesters. You don't get summers off and very few employers are interested in helping you find yourself. Do that on your own time."

Life is very much 24 hours a day and 7 days a week. Spring break, Christmas holiday, summer vacation, teacher planning day…….those go away very quickly once your education has come to its conclusion. Life becomes full time. Expectations become automatic, and legitimate excuses become limited.

Learning to manage your time and your life is your own job. Not a job for your parents, your teachers, your employers, or anyone else. Growing up…..it's a trap, and it's not always pretty. Enjoy being a carefree kid as long as possible.

Rule #10: "Television is not real life. In real life, people actually have to leave the coffee shop and go to jobs."

In the Netflix era, I've been able to watch the sitcom Friends from start to finish, admittedly about five times all the way through now. I get why I love it so much. At the very essence, Friends is about community. Even the theme song…. "I'll be there for you". They had each other, and no outsider was allowed to penetrate their closeness. Despite their own issues with one another from time to time, they had each other's back.

Back to the point though, the Friends characters spent more time chatting, drinking coffee, and socializing, in comparison to going to work, getting an education, or anything else that was of value (some would argue that coffee is pretty valuable).

The reality is that if you want something — you have to work for it. Most of us anyway. We have to get up each and every day, and go to work. We put in long hours, time, devotion, and we make commitments and honor them.

Rule #11: "Be nice to nerds. Chances are you'll end up working for one."

Every time I watch a television show that has a computer expert on it, I'm impressed and amazed; and a little jealous. I wish I knew more about computers and technology. This is what our world revolves around now. Is there anyone who doesn't walk around with a tiny computer, aka cellphone, in their hands or within reach?

Chapter 6
If A Man Wants You

This is an article that I came across back in the 2011-2012 timeframe. I have a link for it; unfortunately, the link is out of date and I can't find the original author.

I was working with a woman, mid-30s, successful in every aspect, beautiful, and yet she was chasing men. Like all of us, she had a good reason. She was using relationships to fill the void that had been created within her from years of neglect and abuse by her parents.

I came across this article and gave it to her. She immediately recognized herself, as well as some behaviors she decided to change. Now obviously this is based on a man; however, it goes both ways.

This what it said;

If a man wants you, nothing can keep him away. If he doesn't want you, nothing can make him stay. Stop making excuses for a man and his behavior. Allow your intuition (or spirit) to save you from heartache. Stop trying to change yourself for a relationship that's not meant to be.

Slower is better. Never live your life for a man before you find what makes you truly happy. If a relationship ends because the man was not treating you as you deserve then, hell no, you can't "just be friends". A friend wouldn't mistreat a friend.

Don't settle. If you feel like he is stringing you along, then he probably is. Don't stay because you think "it will get better." You'll be mad at yourself a year later for staying when things are not better. Don't make plans around theirs, if they want to see you they will.

The only person you can control in a relationship is you. Avoid men who've got a bunch of children by a bunch of different women. He didn't marry them when he got them pregnant, why would he treat you any differently? Always have your own set of friends separate from his. Maintain boundaries in how a guy treats you. If something bothers you, speak up. Never let a man know everything. He will use it against you later. You cannot change a man's behavior. Change comes from within.

Don't EVER make him feel he is more important than you are...even if he has more education or a better job. Do not make him into a god. He is a man, nothing more nothing less. Never let a man define who you are. Never borrow someone else's man. If he cheated WITH you, he'll cheat ON you.

A man will only treat you the way you ALLOW him to treat you. All men are NOT dogs. You should not be the one doing all the bending...compromise is a two-way street.

You need time to heal between relationships. There is nothing cute about baggage. Deal with your issues before pursuing a new relationship.

You should never look for someone to COMPLETE you...a relationship consists of two WHOLE individuals...look for someone complimentary...not supplementary. Dating is fun...even if he doesn't turn out to be Mr. Right.

Make him miss you sometimes...when a man always knows where you are, and you're always readily available to him - he takes it for granted. Never move into his mother's house. Never co-sign for a man. Don't fully commit to a man who doesn't give you everything that you need. Keep him on your radar, but get to know others.

And finally: If you find love let it go...and if it comes back it's yours to keep. Original link http://www.divinecaroline.com/22065/35337-wants

There is some evidence these quotes are attributed to Oprah Winfrey. Just know—this isn't my article and I don't know the exact origin.

Chapter 7
Teenage Pregnancy

There have always been articles and statistics regarding prenatal care for teenagers and other at-risk mothers. There have been numerous government programs put in place, and task-forces established, to address how best to ensure the health of unborn babies and their mothers. I agree this is an important issue and that good health for an infant does start while in utero.

However, I think there is a bigger picture to recognize and address, especially in smaller and more rural communities. Regardless of abstinence programs and contraceptives being readily available, teen pregnancy is at an all-time high. As a social worker and director of an adoption agency, I've seen how an unplanned or crisis pregnancy can affect a teenager and her family.

Unfortunately, shows like "16 and Pregnant" sensationalize teen pregnancy. Though I have not watched the show, I do know that many of these teen moms are on the covers of various magazines and are definitely getting their 15 minutes of fame.

The reality of being a teenage mom is not so glamorous. I recently met with an 18-year old, who delivered twin boys. A product of the foster care system herself, she was sleeping on a friend's couch with her five-pound babies, and the home was infested with roaches. She had quit school in the 10th grade, had no family support, no transportation, and no income. Sadly, she had also buried her 11-month-old daughter due to SIDS, a few months prior to the delivery of these twins. With no job, no income, no education, no transportation, no housing, and no family support, this young girl was still insistent on parenting her young babies.

So many times, in many different communities, young girls find themselves pregnant and are adamant on parenting, regardless of their true ability to do so. Groups of adolescent girls in several places have made the headlines by all intentionally becoming pregnant. Oftentimes, grandparents, and even great grandparents, ultimately end up raising these children born to teen moms. Worse, these babies and children may be abused and neglected, and the Department of Children and Families Services becomes involved (I realize there are exceptions to every situation, and I am generalizing about teen pregnancy).

Adoption is not about giving away a baby. It's about choosing a different path for your infant and yourself. It's about using a difficult situation to improve your life. Adoption is the most selfless act a young and/or ill-prepared mother can choose.

Parenting under the best of circumstances can be difficult. When you try to parent without the needed resources, it causes pain and hardship to both the parents and the child. As parents, educators, and leaders, let's all work together to educate our teens about the reality of parenting and prepare them to just wait!

Chapter 8
Balancing Work And Family:
You Really Can Do It All!

Like most women, for me, the balance of family and career can sometimes feel overwhelming. Here are 5 tips to guarantee success in both areas of your life.

1—Start with routines; when you do the same thing over and over again, not only do you get really good at it, it becomes second nature. You can have several sets of routines for your entire day. Consider having a morning routine, an after-work routine, and/or a bedtime routine. It is helpful to write down everything you do, or need to do, to get to bed at a decent hour, to get out of the house in the morning, and to get dinner on the table quickly and easily. I suggest writing out lists of what needs to be done in each section of your day. As we get older and more forgetful, it is helpful to have a reminder of what needs to be done. When you are rushing around, it is easy to forget something important.

2—Learn to say "NO"— we hear this all the time, but do we practice it? As women, we are people-pleasers and we don't like to upset others, or to feel like we have let someone down. Instead of that, we need to feel the same way about ourselves. Think about how upset you would be if you add one more thing to your "to do" list. Say no for your children as well — don't let them be involved in too many activities.

3—Be sure to schedule appointments to take care of yourself, whatever that might be. Whether it's getting your annual physical, going to the dentist, or meeting your girlfriend for a day at the spa, you have to take care of yourself first in order to properly take care of the other people in your life. This may require creative networking on your part if you have small children. Offering to swap babysitting services with another young mom on your block is often a good start.

4—Exercise has both physical and mental benefits. Even 15 minutes of exercise will cause the brain to release chemicals, which will improve your mood and give you more energy throughout the day. The exercise doesn't have to be strenuous; taking a walk in your neighborhood is a great idea. You may have to put the baby in the stroller or your older child on his/her bicycle. Too often, we don't have to look very hard to find an excuse not to exercise.

5—Use a Master Calendar to keep up with everyone's schedule and appointments. How many times have you missed an event because you forgot or over committed yourself or your family. A master calendar will solve this problem. As soon as you get an invitation, announcement, or other event notice, put it on the calendar right away, and then throw it away! Recording everything you need onto the calendar and throwing away the rest will help to eliminate clutter. Don't stress over what type of calendar to use, just do what works best for you. What you use isn't as important as just using it!

Balancing career and motherhood can be challenging. By implementing these strategies, you will be ahead of the game and enjoying everything that your life has to offer.

Chapter 9
Give Me More

Sometimes people get a case of the gimmes. Give me this, give me that. As Britney Spears sang, "Gimme More". If you've ever raised a child, or especially a teenager, you probably know exactly what I'm referring to. Oftentimes, people are more interested in what they can get from others, as opposed to what they can give. We've all heard the phrase, it's better to give than to receive, but who really practices this anymore?

Despite the fear of showing my age, I can't help but think of the Janet Jackson song "What have you done for me lately?" Why do we continually find ourselves in situations where we are doing all of the giving, or worse, all of the taking? And, let's be honest, who has ever admitted to being a taker? As a mental health clinician, I have never had someone come into my office for counseling and openly admit that they continually take, in some form, from someone they know, or someone they care about.

In this day and age, we have learned to expect instant gratification for almost everything. Get your dry cleaning done today, get your oil changed in 30 minutes, get your glasses done in one hour, freaky fast sandwiches, fast food, lose weight overnight - the list goes on and on.

However, there is one thing that absolutely cannot be done quickly, and that is building a relationship with someone. Whether it's your neighbor, your coworker, your significant other, or anyone else, having a quality relationship with someone takes time to build.

Oftentimes, when I see a couple for marriage counseling, each person is frustrated about what they are not receiving from their partner. Unfortunately, people come into my office and want me to wave a magic wand and make their partner start meeting their needs. Imagine their frustration when I suggest they speak and act in the same ways they want from their partner!

I frequently hear, "Well, why would I do that? I'm so mad and frustrated that I can't do anything for them until I get what I want". Did you ever think that maybe your spouse feels the exact same way as you do? They are equally frustrated with you and cannot fathom meeting your needs until you meet theirs?

At some point, someone has to take the high road, be the bigger person, or whatever cliché you want to use. Why not let it be you? Why not become the giver? Why not be the one that becomes the change you want to see?

What if my spouse doesn't notice? What if they don't reciprocate and pay me back for my kindness? My response is "So what?" Have you become the kind of spouse that only does nice things in the expectation that you will be rewarded? Isn't being nice to your spouse something you've already vowed to do? When was it ever conditional?

On the other hand, let's take the phrase literally. Give me more. You the reader. Give yourself more. More love, more time, more attention. Learn to give to yourself first—way before you give to those around you. This allows you to be able to give more to your partner, your friends, and your family members— if you choose to. Don't let the takers suck you dry. The givers have to set limits, because takers never do.

Set your limits and boundaries today and stick to them. Do be ready for those around to be in shock that they aren't getting their way anymore. That's okay — you're still giving. Only now, you are giving to yourself first. And others, only if you want to.

Chapter 10
The Gun Range

Let me take you back 30+ years ago to July 2013 so that you can understand the significance of this event. As a nine-year-old child, desperate to finish reading a new favorite book, I was hiding in the bathroom, past bedtime. When I left my sanctuary, the place to read peacefully, I was physically attacked and forced up against the bathroom wall towel rack.

The attacker was my 56-year-old father, a World War II and Korean War Veteran, father of three adult children and stepfather to six other children. He was the center of my world, the man who thought I did no wrong. Now, he'd had enough, and when he said go to bed, I was supposed to just do what he said.

But, ah, a nine-year-old who loved to read, up past bedtime. Something so simple, yet it turned out to be the most significant turning point in my entire life. That night began the next five years of vicious physical, emotional, and mental abuse that a child could endure. Oh, I imagine it really had started before that, at least on some level. That night, however, is forever etched in my mind as the beginning.

As a child, I was told "You'll never find a man to love you", "You are fat", "You have ugly hands", "You have the ugliest feet I've ever seen", "You'll never amount to anything", "I hate you", "I'll kill you", "You'll always be a whore, just like your mother", etc. and so forth.

One Sunday morning, when I was 12, I overheard one of the worst conversations. My parents were in the kitchen talking, my mother was baking biscuits and frying sliced potatoes, for tater biscuits. She told my dad about a conversation she and I had had the day prior. During that conversation, I suggested to her she'd like it better if I no longer lived in the house. As she repeated the conversation to him that morning, she added, "It'd be such a blessing to get rid of her". Really, a blessing? That wasn't even a word that we used in our family.

By the age of 14, I was removed from home for the first time and placed in a temporary shelter setting. Eventually, I went to live with an older sister, and one day just decided to move myself back home. Even abused children miss the evil that they know.

Sometime later, my parents divorced, and I was returned to live with my mother. She was considered the nonoffending parent because she had never been physical with me. Despite the divorce, my parents never stopped seeing each other. They were horrible for each other, yet they both realized they weren't fit for anyone else.

One Friday night, in early summer, my dad showed up to drive us to his new home, about an hour away. I refused to go. Even at the young age of 16, I knew what my safety plan read. I didn't need to be around him. I tried to explain this to my parents, but they were unwilling to budge. They insisted that I get in the car with them and go.

After I'd spent some time yelling some pretty vulgar obscenities at my parents, my dad decided that he would ensure that I got in the car that night. I had heard my mother say that he had started keeping a loaded gun under the driver's seat in his car. As he left the front door, to retrieve the gun, he said, "I'm going to put an end to her and her mouth".

Having seen my dad go through fits of uncontrollable rage, I knew better than to stick around and see what might happen. I jumped out my bedroom window, with only the clothes I was wearing, and I hitch-hiked across town. I had one sister that I knew would help me. I got to her house and told her what had happened. She hid me out all weekend, until I could call my social worker on Monday, when I returned to the family-style residential facility that I had called home for the 14 months prior to that night.

Fast forward to today. For 23 years, my startle response has been extremely sensitive. I jumped at the slightest of noises or unexpected movements. I terrified complete strangers as I flailed about from their simple sneezes, coughs, or friendly hellos. I've had an intense, yet understandable, fear of guns.

Everyone has a bucket list, and despite the extreme panic from the sight of a gun, or even just talking about them, I knew that one day I'd overcome it.

I walked into the gun range that day. As is typical with all things men, there was an odd smell, similar to a locker room, full of metal and mildew. The sounds, the bang bang of the guns being fired in the back, came at me without warning. Despite repeatedly startling explosively at times, I continued to listen to what my instructor suggested to me.

I removed my jewelry, and donned my glasses and earmuffs. I followed him through two sets of metal doors, covered with diamond-shaped foam. My skilled and confident instructor put the bullets in the gun clip, showing me each step. He stood by my side, took his time, and spoke slowly and deliberately.

After he set up the target paper, he positioned it 10 yards away. He fired one clip, and I knew that I wouldn't be next. I was ready to leave the moment he aimed and pulled the trigger. As he finished, and prepared the clip for me, I explained that I'd done enough for one day and I was ready to go.

However, with his gentle persuasion and encouragement, I held the gun. I gripped it first with one hand, then the other hand to hold it steady. I felt the cool metal in my hand. I immediately respected the gun, and knew the power that it held. I closed one eye, and took aim. As I began to squeeze the trigger, I held my breath. The first round was out, the second, third, etc.

I went on to fire three full clips onto that paper target. Each time I pulled the trigger, and felt the recoil of the gun, I could physically feel the fear slipping away. The shell casings were popping up at me as I fired. My fearless instructor, right by my side, reminding me to breathe, and pushed me; "do it again, squeeze the trigger".

After the third clip on a fresh target paper for framing, we finished. I walked out of the range, keenly aware that I'd never be the same again. I think I held my head a little higher, and even walked a little more confidently. I knew that I had just overcome my biggest and longest-standing fear. With every bullet fired, that little girl in me let go of the fear, and it was replaced with confidence, strength, and courage.

Chapter 11
Gentle Reminders

Years ago, I had the honor of attending a funeral service for someone that I had only known for a short time. Yet, I learned more about him through his death than I thought possible.

David was a simple man who lived a simple life. He and his wife of 47 years had four sons, and five grandchildren. He didn't have great wealth and didn't drive expensive cars. He didn't have a prestigious career. So, what did he have? What made him so special?

Life is all about rituals. We perform them to finish an education, to start a life with a spouse, to celebrate the life of a new baby. So many times, however, funerals are overlooked as the ritual we use to memorialize and say goodbye.

I watched and stood by at the wake, as hundreds of people came through to honor and give remembrance to David. For most of the time, the line of people was out the door and into the parking lot. The long line and steady stream of people continued for nearly 4 hours.

One by one, they all shared their memories of David, and everyone had a story to tell. I heard of how he had given money to a young groom who wasn't making very much and felt down and out. I heard the story about how David drove an hour out of his way to pick up a pair of shoes that a young lad had forgotten at the school. I heard the hilarious tale of how he had fallen while hanging blinds and had to be taken to the emergency room by two of his sons. I heard dozens of stories about how David had flirted with all of the ladies he came across. I heard the story of how David had the ritual of going to the local Depot each morning. I heard about how David always drove the school bus and how the children simply adored him.

Dozens of people shared how they had only just seen him in the community in recent months, and that he had made no mention of his illness or his long stays in the hospital. Doctors and nurses who cared for him during his many illnesses came to pay their respects. The Hospice staff came, his children's friends came, his relatives came, neighbors came, and his wife's coworkers came. There were numerous flower arrangements, monetary gifts, and plaques in his honor.

I was reminded of many things by being a part of the ceremonies. Social Work is a well-known, and respected, profession and academic discipline. Social Workers obtain an education, often an advanced degree, and a state license. The goal of a social worker is to, "do no harm", and improve the quality of life and wellbeing of others. It's about teaching, protecting, and serving. David had no degree in social work, but he had a social worker's heart. He gave all that he had, at times sacrificing himself for others. He sought to make others smile with his stories and good-natured fun. He lived for the moments he could spend with his grandchildren. He attended their sporting events, birthday parties, and was a part of their everyday lives.

David lived with honor, gave when he had nothing to give, and loved all those around him. He also lived by example. He was a little fish in his pond, but he made his presence a big one by being humble, gentle, and kind. I know his legacy lives on in his four sons. Most importantly, he reminded me, in his death, that smiles are free and a kind word doesn't cost a thing, but the lasting effects are priceless.

*Name changed to protect privacy.

Dr. Tracy Riley

Chapter 12
Things I Have Learned While Being In 7th Grade As A 39-Year-Old Mom Of Three Teenagers

I had the privilege of shadowing my 13-year-old son recently at Mayport Middle School. It was the easiest thing to schedule, I simply called the school and asked. The answer was an immediate yes. All of the teachers were informed in advance of my visit to their classroom.

Why did I call and ask if I could do this? Well........ya see..... There are two teachers that regularly take the time to inform me of my son's behavior problems and poor grades. I greatly appreciate them keeping me informed. However, my son has tried to convince me that these teachers hate him, and it's their "fault" that his grades are bad.

Since I'm much more old school than I like to admit, and I call his reasoning "bull something" or other, I thought I'd handle it my way instead. I had nothing else to do that day anyway (please note the sarcasm).

It is an understatement to say that things have changed in the last 30+ years since I attended 7th-grade full time.

Teachers are responsible for walking the students everywhere they go. That includes supervised trips to the bathroom, and walking them to each class. There is also an order to the line, as boys and girls cannot walk together. They must be segregated into their respective gender groups.

There are no lockers. Actually, that's not true. There are lockers, but they are not utilized by the students. The lockers are just there, all with locks on them. Students are given certain textbooks to take home, and use others while in the classroom.

Our first class was Civics. The information covered in this class was quite interesting. The teacher discussed *Propaganda and Political Parties*. She was easily able to hold the students' attention, and explained the information on a basic, simple to understand, level. I did notice that taking notes is not like it used to be. Back in my day, I didn't have a phone that would snap a picture of the slide the teacher presented. I had to use my pen and paper, and actually write down the information.

Next up, we head to Health. Of course, the Civics teacher walked us there, while bumping into numerous other lines of segregated boys and girls in the hallways. Once seated, and quiet, in this class the teacher explained the change from the Food Pyramid to the Plate. This was a much larger classroom, but this teacher rocked when it came to keeping the students quiet, respectful, and paying attention. She also did a review of an upcoming test and helped them to feel prepared for that.

Now is a really good time to mention that both teachers mistook me for a student. I'm wearing jeans and three-inch heels. A student? Oh, for nothing in this world would I want to be a student in middle school again!

During Health we were given a bathroom break, as students are not allowed to go during the class change time. That would disrupt the line from class to class, and apparently, students cannot be unsupervised. I was grateful for the bathroom break, and even more grateful to get to use the teacher's lounge!

After Health, my son and I darted out to grab lunch at a local restaurant. Going to school is challenging enough, but there is no way that I'm brave enough to go to the cafeteria.

After lunch, we headed to Science. This teacher is adorable, she's young and energetic, and looks to be about as young as her students. Apparently, my young lad sits all alone at a table in the back of the room. This is one of the classes where his behavior needs significant improvement. According to this adorable teacher, he chooses to sit alone to minimize his distractions.

I would be remiss if I didn't point out that I took full advantage of every opportunity to embarrass him today. I gave him hugs, I kissed his cheek, I had him carrying my stuff, I called him by my favorite nicknames "Boo Boy" and "Little Man", and of course, I announced to everyone possible that he's my son and we are spending the day together. Nothing fazed him in the least. He didn't care that I was with him, and almost relished in the extra attention. My plan backfired.

His behavior in my presence wasn't really that great. I was embarrassed that he called his classmates negative names, talked too much, didn't pay attention, and was just goofy. However, even with all of those behaviors, he was one of the better behaved kids in the class.

After Science, with only one hour remaining, I rushed out. I had to get back to my adult world, with access to the internet, and the opportunity to go to the bathroom whenever I wanted. I definitely enjoyed 7th grade much more this time than I did 25 years ago. With that being said, I never want to go back. Oh, and I'm absolutely certain that my career choice was perfect for me. These teachers are the closest thing to angels that I've ever seen.

As a side note—that was many years ago. Wesley is now an adult, exploring college opportunities and has grown into the most wonderful young man I could have imagined. We still laugh about our day together in 7th grade.

Chapter 13
Positive Parenting--5 Surefire Ways to Improve Your Parenting Style

What are some of the best things about being a parent? If you are like me, you can fill up an hour talking about all the good things that come from being a parent. When parenting becomes most difficult, it is helpful to refer back to our list of these things to remind us of how great it is, or can be. Take a few minutes now and create a list of all of the great things that come to your mind about parenting your child or children. You can even do a separate list for each child and another list that encompasses all of your children.

There are many external factors that parents must deal with today. Parents must contend with their child's peers and the pressures that can bring. The media exposure through television and music can also conflict with the positive message parents are trying to bring to their children. A parent's work schedule may make it difficult to spend quality time together as a family. There are always factors that we must overcome if we are to parent our children in a positive and uplifting manner.

Here are five ways to improve your parenting style and bring back closeness with you and your child.

Some of these tips are not for the faint of heart—parenting requires hard work and dedication to the task at hand. I can assure you that these tips are tried and true in my home.

1—Routines: When children know what to expect, they are able to practice making good decisions based on the continuity of a routine. Families should have several sets of routines, carried out throughout the day. Morning routines get us up on time and out the door, after school routines ensure all homework is done, and the most important routine is the one that is done before going to bed.

Here are some ideas of what to include in your routines. We'll start with the most important one:

> Before Bed routine, which actually starts right after the evening meal, will include getting ready for the next day. It will consist of getting a bath, brushing your teeth, and laying out clothes for the next day. This helps adults as well as children. If you find what you want to wear has a button missing or a

stain, you can easily make the decision to repair or wash your item, or pick something else (have you ever tried to figure out what to wear when you got up late and have to be out the door in five minutes only to find your favorite blouse has a stain on it?). Also, before bed, ensure that anything that needs to get out the door with you in the morning is packed and ready to go, including lunch or lunch money, the backpack with homework and permissions slips. If you eat breakfast at home, this is a great time to set the table and put out the cereal box.

Morning routine—when morning comes around there is no thinking needed—the clothes are ready and laid out, the bag is packed, and you can move right into the basics of the breakfast, getting dressed, brushing teeth and getting out the door in time without a frantic rush or panicking because you forgot something important.

After School or Afternoon Routine—this can be for your children or for you if you stay home with younger children. For school-aged children, when they come in from school, this is the time for snacks, chores, and starting homework. This is especially important if you aren't home, because they know exactly what needs to be done and they can get started on it so that it is done. This then allows you to easily move into the next set of routines after the evening meal. If you are a stay at home mom, the afternoon is the time when you will want to make sure you have a plan for dinner, if you haven't exercised yet, do you have a plan to? Have you had something for lunch?

The importance of the routines is to look at what you and your family do each day to get out the door on time and get to bed at a decent hour. It helps to write everything down until it becomes...well...routine for you. It is different for every family, but here is an example of our routines. (My husband and I are raising five children together, ages 8, 9, 11, 14 and 16. The following routines primarily apply to the youngest three)

Before bed—clothes are selected based on the weather; each child takes a shower and brushes their teeth. Each child is encouraged to read for 20 minutes, usually with Mom or Dad. Bedtime is 8:30.

Morning—each child gets up at 7:30 and gets dressed, has breakfast of cereal and fruit, and brushes their hair and teeth. Our youngest must take medication and put in her contacts. Any additional time is used to read, start on the afternoon chores, or tidy up their room. We are out the door at 8:20 for the bus.

After school—each child has a snack, does afternoon chores, and completes their homework. Any time after that and before dinner, can be used to play outside, or, if they have earned it, they can have 30 minutes to play games on the computer.

(You may notice there is no television time mentioned. I will cover this more in tip #5.)

2—Spend time with your child each day doing something meaningful; children spell love as TIME. Depending on your child's age, pick an appropriate activity such as reading a book, playing outside, or helping with homework. I don't consider or recommend watching television as a meaningful activity, as there is no interaction with your child (more on this in tip #5).

Spending time with your child isn't really optional if you want to be a positive parent. If all you ever say to them is "hurry up", "don't do that", "stop", "why didn't you.....", you will quickly become a nag and they will tune you out, as well as everything you say to them, good or bad. Take the time to do something with them, and if you have more than one, you may have to schedule fun time with each of them. It's easy to get caught up in the business of getting everything done, but I promise, you will not send them off to college wishing you had washed more dishes.

3—Part of spending time with your child is eating a meal together at least five nights a week. It's amazing how much you can learn from your child over a meal. Children want to tell you about their day. They want to know someone is interested in them. Start this as early as possible, even if your child is still in a high chair. Pull it up to the table and make it a family event.

I have a 14-year-old and I've been doing this since she was 2 years old. As I had more children, we continued the tradition of asking each other two questions each night. We call it "Best Thing/Worst Thing". We each share the best thing and worst thing that happened to us during the day. The best thing is an opportunity for everyone to share some of their achievements of the day and it gives the parents an opportunity to praise their child for making good decisions. The worst thing allows the child to share any struggles or issues and helps them to learn that Mom and Dad and home are safe places to talk about their issues or concerns. This also allows the child a chance to process what happened and what they might have been able to have done differently to achieve an alternative and more positive outcome.

4—Know your child's friends—this becomes more and more important as they get older. How do you do this? Let your house be the one that the kids want to come to. Have snacks available to them, food will almost always attract the kids, especially the teenagers. Give them a place to just hang out, watch television, get on social media, or listen to music. Make it as supervised as possible, without being obvious. Our teenagers do not go to someone else's home unless I know and have talked with the parents to ensure that an adult will be home.

By letting my children's friends come to our house, it gives me a chance to see how these young people conduct themselves and I can decide if I want their influence on my child. My children know our values and if they bring someone home that doesn't share a closeness to our values, I discourage the friendship. Youth who come to our house and help themselves to our refrigerator or pantry without permission are not usually invited back. I also use this as a teaching opportunity for my children; appropriate behavior when you are a guest in someone's home.

5—Turn off the television and keep it off. Did I hear a gasp yet? When I say turn off the television, I mean turn it off for five days out of the week. There are several reasons that I suggest this. By the time the kids get home from school, and complete their afternoon routines of homework, snack, and chores, it is usually getting close to dinner time. Between a day at school and their afternoon responsibilities, they need some fresh air, some exercise, and just some down-time in general. How relaxing is it to sit and color, or talk on the phone with their friends, or even better, let them help prepare dinner with you, which is a perfect example of tip #2. After the evening meal, you are starting your before-bed routine, and getting ready for the next day, then it's bedtime.

Another reason to turn off the television is the shows that are on today. It's not Mayberry or Pollyanna that our kids are being exposed to. If you have watched any of the shows on Disney lately, you will see that the kids are in control, parents are either absent or absolutely clueless about what their children are doing. There is usually some form of deception involved, a lie is told and the kids spend 30 minutes trying to cover it up, instead of just being honest upfront. Is this the message you want to send to your child?

Reality shows, such as "Sweet 16" portray teenagers celebrating this monumental milestone, thinking they deserve a $50,000 car in the color of their choice. And the parents oblige! Do you plan to drop that much money on any of your children's birthdays? It's very difficult to have your children buy into your values, morals, and beliefs while letting them have exposure to beliefs that differ so greatly.

In our home, the television can be turned on for pre-approved shows on Friday nights and Saturdays only. By Sunday afternoon, we are in 'getting ready for the week' mode, so we keep it off unless there is something in particular that would be a treat for all of us to enjoy together. My 9-year-old is in a class with 23 other students and he is one of only two children who don't watch television on school nights.

Many times parents want to blame our schools, churches, and neighborhoods for the way our children are being raised. It's time that we as parents fully accept our responsibility for the fate of our children.

I made the choice to have my children and I believe that it is 100% my responsibility to train them in the way they should go. You would not take a young plant, one that doesn't yet have strong and firm roots and leave that plant in the dead of winter without protection. Children are not "little adults", their minds are not developed. We have to protect them, make decisions for them, and all along the way teach them the way they should go, so that when the time is right, adulthood happily awaits them.

Chapter 14
Grief Dreams

Just this week, I was talking with Larry, a high school classmate, who shared with me that he had been having several dreams about his late wife. She had suddenly died early last fall at a very young age, leaving him behind with an infant son. As Larry and I talked, he admitted that these dreams were upsetting to him. He hadn't dreamed about her in many months.

I know that dreams are a normal part of the healing process. I explained to him how dreams are the mind's way of processing our loss, and trying to make sense of a senseless situation. In my nightly reading, I came across some additional thoughts I want to share.

A dream may manifest as a searching for the person who died. Perhaps you dream that you are in a crowded room and can't find your loved one. It seems unfair, that you are experiencing the loss again and again. Even in your sleep, you have to experience the loss, and you might feel powerless to stop it, just as in reality.

Dreams also provide several opportunities. You might have a need to feel closer to the person who died. Perhaps your mind is trying to accept the reality of that person's death. Oftentimes, our subconscious enjoys renewing the memories that made that person so special in the first place.

Another opportunity our dreams can offer could be a chance to resolve unfinished business. If the death occurred without warning, and there wasn't a chance to say goodbye, your subconscious could be attempting to make peace.

Dreams can also show you a hope for the future, especially if your loved one gives you permission to move forward.

The content of your dreams often reflects changes as you progress on your grief journey. It's important to find a skilled listener, who will simply listen without interpreting your dreams.

However, if you are not dreaming about your lost loved one, that's okay too. Your grief journey is unique to you and depends on many factors. Do not feel slighted for not having dreams. No two people will grieve the same, and grieving differently just reaffirms that we are all different and unique, just like our loved ones.

Chapter 15
Eating Out With the Kids....Do You Dare?

Does the thought of taking your kids to a sit-down restaurant make you cringe? For the purposes of this chapter, a sit-down restaurant doesn't include those with stars next to the name of the restaurant. We are just talking about your average family-oriented restaurant.

A few months ago, my cousin and I were meeting for dinner. We hadn't seen each other in years and we were both excited about getting together. At the time, her son was just under two. She was extremely hesitant to go anywhere that didn't involve the meal being delivered in a wrapper with a toy. Because my children are older, I was surprised at her hesitation. She suggested several times that we just eat in at her house—my thoughts were about letting someone else do the cooking, and the cleaning, for the meal!

As it turned out, we went to a local buffet restaurant and, with the exception of my nine-year-old accidentally dropping his entire tray on the floor, the meal was uneventful. Her son got a little antsy near the end, but it was late and getting close to his bedtime anyway. The evening got me thinking about other restaurant experiences where the children were more noticeable than the main course.

If your child is young and small enough to still be in an infant carrier, you can probably make it through most meals with relatively few issues. Timing, though, is always important with infants. You will want to get the baby fed and happy before your meal arrives, if you still enjoy eating a hot meal.

Timing also applies to a child that sits in a high chair during the meal. It usually helps to have favorite toys, books, and extra snacks for a high chair child. Most restaurants will supply crayons and coloring sheets, but how many one and two-year-olds do you know that wouldn't eat the crayon?

Teaching a child how to have proper table manners begins at home. You can't let a young child run around all day with food in their hands and then expect them to sit down at a restaurant and wait good-naturally. Having sit-down meals at home will help a child "practice" their restaurant manners. By the time your child is four, they should be able to wait patiently for the food, while being entertained with books, games, or activities.

What do you do if something goes wrong? Let's face it, even with the best planning your child may be having an off day. You may not even realize it until the order is placed. If a meltdown is approaching, you may have to take your child outside for a few minutes. The worst thing you can do is to do nothing and let him disturb or distract others. The second worst thing you can do is to give your child something you wouldn't normally give them, just to get them quiet. Don't let now be the time you hand over your cell phone, or enormous metal key chain, to calm them down. Guess what happens the next time they can't be calmed down in a normal manner?

Recently, I was enjoying dinner at a restaurant that also houses a country store on the other side of the building. There was a child, probably about four years old. He came in with his family, in the middle of a full-blown tantrum. What appeared to be his grandmother walked the child out of the restaurant and when they returned they were empty-handed. The child continued to scream and cry, so grandmother again took the child out of the restaurant and into the store. The second time they returned, the child had 3 new toys from the store. What was Grandma thinking? Why would anyone reward this type of behavior?

Having kids doesn't mean you can't leave home for an enjoyable meal out. It just involves proper planning, clear expectations, and a back-up plan for the unexpected. Proper planning starts at home—no matter what the situation. Parenting is fun, and the unexpected is often part of that fun. Other parents have been where you are, and it will fly by sooner than you think.

Chapter 16
Marriage and Relationships...Is it Self or Service and are You Ready?

Anytime you are considering a commitment such as marriage, love can blind you to reality. As we all know, over 50% of marriages end in divorce. That rate is even higher for second and third marriages. It is important to go into any relationship with your eyes wide open.

Often times, the "real" person you are dating does not show up right away. He/she sends their best representative to the relationship. It is imperative that you know the real person you want to commit to, and not the person you think they are. This requires spending time together, having open and honest communication, and not rushing any decisions about a future together.

Topics to openly discuss and hopefully agree on prior to marriage include finances, child-rearing, extended family relations, and the division of household duties. As a family therapist, I recommend putting pen to paper and making sure that these are areas that you can agree on prior to saying "I do". Think about the details. If family is a first priority, how will these things change if one parent stays home to care for the children? If both parents continue working, what will the child care plan be?

Don't be fooled by large promises, if there is no evidence to support such a claim early in the relationship. A guy who lives like a slob isn't going to suddenly become neat just because someone else is around who likes everything neat and orderly. Someone who spends money impulsively may have a difficult time reining in that spending habit.

People have said to me "I don't know who I am married to, it's like we never dated". Too many times, people enter a marriage with the idea of changing their partner. As you may already know, this rarely happens successfully. Rather than focusing on what the other person can do to make the relationship better, you will have to focus on yourself instead. The reality is that you are the only one that you can change.

Relationships do take work. Marriage should not be described as a 50/50 endeavor, but rather two people giving 100% of themselves to the relationship. At times, one or the other may have to give what seems like more than 100%. There may be times when it seems that all you do is give to the other person. If you notice these patterns before marriage, take note. Someone who is used to receiving may not want to start giving in return.

Today's society continues to be geared towards what we can get from others. It is vital to focus on what you can give to your significant other, when entering a relationship or wanting to see change for the better. Focusing on someone else can give you a sense of fulfillment that focusing on yourself will never provide.

When considering marriage, be prepared to lose a little of self, invest in another person, and watch a dynamic duo emerge. If possible, seek assistance from a trusted friend or parent who has been married for many years. Arguments and disagreements are unavoidable at times, but, with proper planning and a strong commitment, your marriage can be hugely successful. You can add to the statistics for having a lengthy relationship—not one ending in divorce.

Chapter 17
One-Liners

The title of this book has been in the works for many years. Quite some time ago, I started sharing little things I would hear during therapy sessions. I used social media as my outlet to do said sharing, and began calling it, "Tales from the Couch", in order to catch the reader's attention. Most of this chapter is one-liners that I heard while counseling, doing trainings, or working with fellow therapists in some other form.

As stated before, enough of the details have been changed to avoid any identifying information of the person sharing. These are shared from over the last 20 years, in no particular order. To further ensure anonymity, I asked other therapists to share their funny stories through the years.

Adult One-Liners

Client: Last night I had a threesome with my son and his therapist.

Me: We call that family therapy here, NOT a threesome.

Client: Male client shared that he was asked out by another man and he's not gay. His response: I'm sure you're lovely, but I like girls.

Therapist: What are you doing today to make your tomorrow better?

Client: Not a Damn Thing.

Client: I don't care if I get the Coronavirus, I just want to go to the casino and get out of the house.

Client: Do tinfoil hats attract aliens?

Client: Where is Maslow? He's the main reason I come here.

Client: Dr. Riley, you're not married or dating are you? That's got to be the reason you're always happy.

Client: I brought wine for today's session, we are going to need it.

Client: I took my cat for a walk…..in a stroller.

Client: You're my rent-a-friend.

Client: I think you're a hot babe, but I will stick to the professional boundaries you have set.

Client: My wife thinks you're beautiful, so I need you to refer me to another therapist.

Client: I am dog sitting for my wife's boyfriend, but she doesn't know that I know it's her boyfriend.

Client: My husband is going to escort websites, but he's not really meeting up with them.

Client: This stripper really liked me, I think she was into me.

Therapist: Seriously? She did her job well then.

Therapist: Tell me about your week

Client: My greatest accomplishment is not correcting grammar and spelling on social media.

Therapist: Win!

Client: You and the Amazon delivery driver are the only people I am seeing this week. I am in my cocoon, and I like it that way.

Therapist: (At the start of couple's counseling) Let's talk about your relationship and ways you can show one another love.

Wife: I really don't want to talk about loving him; I don't like him.

Client: Therapy is mental milk of magnesia. I'm not stuck anymore. Talking to you is like when you're constipated and you go exercise. It shakes things loose.

Therapist: That's a shitty comparison, but I like it.

Therapist: You are 27, why are you wearing a onesie; and in public?

Client: I don't mean to be rude, but how old are you?
Therapist: I am 40.

Client: You don't even look close to 30.

Therapist: Thank you!

Client: It wasn't a compliment.

Client: Why am I so against getting engaged to my girlfriend?

Therapist: Why would you be against touching a hot stove?

Client: Because I would get burned.

Therapist: Bingo!

Client: You'll be so proud of me — I went to a gay bar this weekend!

Client: I sure am glad you're fat; I could never trust a skinny therapist.

Client: I have 8 different personalities and none of them like you.

Therapist: Do you have pain anywhere?

90-year-old client: Yes, my pussy aches.

Client: Where do you think you're going being so tall?

Therapist: Pretty much everywhere. I'm 5'10.

Therapist: Do you ever hear voices in your head that aren't yours?

Client: Doesn't everybody?

Client tests positive for marijuana and says: It's a false positive because of ibuprofen.

Client comes in, looks around, and asks: Did you go to school for this?

Client: I am dating my mom's ex-boyfriend. I need you to help me tell her.

Client: My first wife looked like a model, she was gorgeous. But when I got diagnosed with mental illness, she left me. Now, my second wife, she's not beautiful like my first wife. She's just regular, you know, she's like you. But that's okay, because you're both pretty on the inside.

Children One-Liners

12-year-old client with Oppositional Defiant Disorder: As my therapist, you are a fuckity-fuck.

Therapist documentation: Client called therapist a fuckity-fuck; will continue to monitor.

6-year-old client to in home therapist: You're as ugly as Tinkerbell.

5-year-old client, walking behind therapist: Your butt is big.

9-year-old client: I am really into rocks and stuff; not like crack or anything. I just really like rocks.

8-year-old client: Are you fat or pregnant?

4-year-old client: I could beat you down easily.

12-year-old client: You are torture to talk to.

3-year-old client at a sand table wiggling around....

Therapist: Do you need to go to the bathroom?

3-year-old client: No, my butt is just wiggly.

7-year-old client: I have difficulty regulating my emotions, and sometimes I just need a break.

6-year-old client: Do you have on makeup?

Therapist: Yes I do.

6-year-old client: You look like a dog.

8-year-old client: You're the sweetest white person I know.

14-year-old client: You're a psychotherapist....spelled "PSYCHO THE RAPIST", you're like a mind raper.

8-year-old client: You kind of suit being fat, like I don't think I'd look good as a fat person, but you do.

6-year-old client: Do you live in your car like my other worker does?

6-year-old client: You would look terrible if you were bald.

Just as a reminder, these things are not shared as a way to be mean, criticize, or demean anyone's choice for choosing therapy. I share these things as a way to normalize therapy. It's much like any regular conversation you have with anyone (except that therapy is a one sided conversation about only you).

Therapy is hard work, and some sessions are difficult to experience, regardless of which chair you are sitting in— either as the therapist or the individual attending the session.

Being a therapist means we never know what we are going to hear that day. Is someone suicidal? Getting divorced? Celebrating a new job? We never know what to expect.

But we are human, and it's important to be able to laugh with others as they laugh, and cry (not literally) as they cry.

A good therapist will hold up a mirror so you can see yourself more clearly, while at the same time removing distortions and judgments. This mirror is one of compassion and love. There is no need to cringe when you view yourself through this glass. The reflection becomes objective, allowing you to take note of what changes you want to make.

Other people in your life can hold the mirror up for you. However, because they don't want to upset you, they will tilt it, to allow only the good stuff to be reflected. While it may feel good for a moment, it ends up doing more harm than good. It does not help if you are truly wanting to learn about yourself and make positive changes.

Chapter 18
Are You Using Your Remote Control?

Most of us encounter situations where we need to take a step back and reflect upon our lives. We need to weigh the consequences of our past actions and the coming blessings the future holds for us. There are moments when you feel like your world is spinning, where there's too much to do and you don't have a clue where to begin; when there's a lot holding you down and you don't think you can get up. This is the time to take control of your life, stir things up knowing you're the one in charge.

Life is so much like a remote control. The buttons on the device represent every aspect of our lives. Think about it; we play, we pause, we stop, and sometimes we simply rewind and start over. We can use the volume and the brightness buttons to make adjustments. Sometimes we power down and start all over the next day, or after a vacation.

Monitor the volume! Who are you listening to?

It's common knowledge that it's important to keep good energy around you. There's a lot of YouTube videos talking about "good vibes" and repelling "negative energy", but do we really get the message? People generally are inherently biased towards their friends and loved ones, especially when they're kind and loving. We usually want to see them as good people, but that does not mean their opinions and advice are what we should follow all the time. Many times, we tend to think the attitude of people close to us does not really affect us, but it does!

Have you ever tried doing a project with a lazy pessimist? Going through such an experience will definitely make people more self-conscious, and willing to filter the advice and opinions from friends, loved ones, and even acquaintances. While teammates will see such a person as a negative individual who seems to feel the project will fail, that person is also someone's friend, brother, or sister. There are people that cherish that person and feel they have the best intentions towards them, which they do.

However, their view of the world is negative, and the ideas you pick up from such a person would not necessarily be good for you. It is, therefore, crucial to be careful of the attitude of the people you listen to, no matter your disposition towards them. Sometimes even a foe with the right attitude is worth listening to. So I'll ask again: who are you listening to?

Zoom in: What's the big thing in your lens?

Have you ever been caught in a situation where you're spread too thin, juggling 20 things at once? When you're caught in a mire, sometimes it's difficult to see straight. Many times we lose sight of what matters, of why we're even doing everything, because of the minor details. Sometimes, we lose sight of family, friends, and other things that really matter, all because we're dead set on chasing too many rabbits. All you need to do is breathe in deeply, exhale, and repeat. I mean this figuratively of course.

You need to stop for a moment and think about what's really important, about the choices that need to be made for you to be centered, because you really can't win everything, and then try to execute that. As the saying goes, "He who chases two rabbits catches none". Pick your war, and never zoom out from your major focus, even if it means losing some peripheral battles.

Turn up the brightness--are you having dark thoughts?

It's tough when nothing works out. It's tough when we fail over and over again. It's tough dealing with a broken heart and failed relationships. There are a million more reasons why being human in the 21st century, and since the beginning of time, can be tough. There are times we feel sad, lonely, and even empty. Sometimes we might even just want to stop breathing when we feel the weight of the world crushing our lungs. Today I'll say, "Hold on". That's really all I have to say on that.

You just need to persevere, not because it will soon be over, that may not be the case. Hold on because you never know what will come later. You don't know who you will meet tomorrow who may change the way you look at one thing, or your whole outlook. It does not get emphasized enough, but the people you surround yourself with may not always be the best company for you. In too many cases, we are too complacent and sensitive to be around the people we actually need to be around. Even having the right people around does not mean there will be no more sad days or no more getting depressed. That may still happen, but the way you climb out of it and the processes that go on in your head are greatly affected by the people around you.

Sometimes, we have loving and supporting friends who never tell us the bitter truth because of how it will make us feel. We may have people who put us on a pedestal, or even people who are extremely harsh and judgmental towards us. The point is these things can affect our general outlook and may also affect the way we process situations.

I have witnessed, many times, two people processing the exact same circumstances in totally opposing manners. One person got very down and wasn't motivated to do anything. The other person got very down and sad as well, and, although it took some days, that other person resolved to move on, despite the odds being stacked against them. That comparison is highly subjective and depends solely on a person's mentality, which is what I'm driving at here. It's all about the way we process things. While we can't all fit into a "happy go lucky" personality bracket, what we can do is to hold on.

I had the experience where one person's casual phrasing actually changed my outlook when I was in a tough spot. He was groping through the same things as I was, and things were really tough. I saw the situation as difficult, impossible, and draining. My friend described the situation as, *"rather challenging"*. It is almost unbelievable how these words changed my outlook. Yes, the situation was incredibly difficult for him too, but the difference is you can't win in an impossible situation, but you can overcome a challenge. To date, that friend does not know how he changed my outlook on life. After all, all he said was "challenging".

Stop--Abort the mission

Nothing, I repeat, nothing is worth you sacrificing your health over. At the end of the day, while pushing yourself hard will get the job done, being sick or suffering from major health issues as a result of heaping too much on your shoulders does not do anybody any good. It would not help to be sick and unproductive at a job you overwork yourself for. If the situation is bad for your physical health and mental wellbeing, I have only one thing to say; pack up your bags, and get away from there as fast as you can. The people who will argue that "it's not always as simple as that" are correct, but mark my words: It will be worth it.

Pause--Take a break.

Stop and smell the roses. Yes, our days are busy. We have to work crazy hours, and there's just so much to do with so little time. However, sometimes we just need a dose of fresh air. We need to step back, take in the world around us, and soak it in. So every once in a while, when you're rushing to the office, or contemplating how you're going to get through a stressful week, stop and smell the roses, or lilies if you want. The choice of flower is not important. What is important is that you employ any method you think is fit for this purpose. You can go running, take a day off, meditate, do yoga, go hiking, anything you want. It's your day!

Rewind—look from the vantage point

Our decisions lead to the situations we find ourselves in, and sometimes we feel angry or frustrated and wonder, how did we end up here? We ponder where we might have gone wrong in the past. We try to retrace our steps and try to relive those moments, then imagine a better scenario if a better or different decision had been made at one point in time.

However, the details are in the little things. We may look back on what happened, but the important thing here is to try learning from our past. We can separate our mind from ourselves and objectively judge ourselves like a stranger.

Take many steps back, be as far from yourself and your thought making process as possible, and you'll begin to spot the devil in the details. Take a step back, assess, learn, and then soldier on.

Power down—Just get out of it.

There's a proverb I heard once that succinctly summarizes everything I'll say here. It says, "the more you look, the less you see". While it sounds so banal, we can consider its effectiveness in so many areas of wellbeing. "The more you look, the less you see".

This effect can even be noticed in academics. There are many reports of people getting to an answer when they are not actually working on a problem. Sometimes this happens because we spend too much time on a problem. We become myopic and mentally drained due to that problem. However, when we step away, our horizon broadens and we can begin to see the full picture. Sometimes all we need is rest and all of a sudden, all is right with the world again.

Play- wake up inner child, wake up!

To some people, this is a dog-eat-dog world and they come ready for the fight. Others, not so much, and some cannot even acknowledge anything is going on. This is of course due to different individual backgrounds. Many of us, be it athletes, blue or white collar workers, or students, have a chip on our shoulder and fight daily to prove something, or to make ends meet. All these are important, but there's something that can be forgotten in that pursuit; our happiness.

Do you remember the carefree days of childhood? Do you remember when you weren't chasing bills, or had too many responsibilities? Do you remember how much fun it was to let go and play? Looking back now, those games might seem silly, but it's the action I'm referring to, the ability to turn a set of mundane activities into fun, lots of fun, and keep coming back to it. For example, some childhood games involved jumping rope. The exact same activity is done in the gym, yet there is a different feel to it.

Yet, when children, there was some sort of fun activity with weird rules. We ran about chasing each other without having to be bothered about the duration of our 100-meter sprint. We jumped on the trampolines because there's some danger once you leave the ground and its fun! Most of you reading this should be able to relate to this, and more. The point I want to drive home here is sometimes bring your inner child back. Don't let your day-to-day be the reason you forget yourself, or forget you need to be happy too. Sometimes, despite the mundaneness of it all, bring back your inner child, and define your own version of fun.

Change the channel- Don't be afraid to redefine YOU

FDR is quoted as saying, "The only thing we have to fear is fear itself". I totally get the merit of this, but I beg to differ.

You can quote me on this; "the only thing we have to fear is ourselves". Confused? Befuddled? Let me explain.

Each of us has tremendous potential; however, where a lot of things go awry is in the implementation. Can you imagine what you could have achieved if you'd never let fear stand in your way? What might happen if you did not overthink something that you thought was a golden idea from the get-go? The moment things get critical, if you just let yourself go full throttle, without succumbing to your weaknesses, many of you can achieve your potential. The point of this is not to berate you. I know it's easier said than done to get things done the way you envisioned them, but really, we are our own biggest obstacles. To win on the outside, we have to be victorious within.

Everything I've written so far has been geared towards this, including; mind who you're listening to, take a break, let it be, and just free yourself. These are at the heart of my message. All I've been trying to say is, I know life can be rough. I know it can be tough. For some people, the expectations of their everyday life are tough and really unbelievable. I don't want you to neglect your duties, but, also, I don't want you to neglect yourself. Never feel like you're less than extraordinary, and never let anyone treat you as such.

Many of us know what to do to make ourselves happy. However, the fear of making that leap, the fear of the change, and how other people might take it, the fear of not getting accepted, the fear of losing friends if you go through with it, also comes with these decisions. They are definitely not easy ones to make. If you find yourselves at such a point, you can choose not to make the change for any number of reasons, but let none of them be fear! Never be afraid to change you.

Chapter 19
Live It, Own It, Act It

People attend therapy for many different reasons. If the therapist takes the position of being in charge and knowing it all, it's not as helpful for the client. Now, of course the therapist is an expert, but not necessarily THE expert.

I always explain to the individuals that come to see me that they are the expert on themselves. I want to learn about them, from them. Not from a place of judgment or criticism. I want the individuals sitting on my couch to teach me. I'll take my newfound knowledge of them, add in my expertise in a particular area, and help them see things in a brand new way.

Many people have the assumption that therapists give advice, or tell you what to do. That is an incorrect expectation. Therapists listen intensely first. In fact, we are even taught how to listen in school. Over the years, here are some things that I have learned from the people sitting on my couch. I learned to listen so I could learn how to help others.

A few of my favorite quotes on listening:

> Most of the successful people I've known are the ones who do more listening than talking. –Bernard Baruch

> Listening is often the only thing needed to help someone. –Anonymous

> Listen. People start to heal the moment they feel heard. –Cheryl Richardson

> Most people do not listen with the intent to understand; they listen with the intent to reply. –Stephen Covey

> When you talk, you are only repeating what you already know. But if you listen, you may learn something new. –Unknown

The Body Talks

While we are on the subject of listening, it's important to note that the body has all the answers, if only we would listen to it. If we get cold, we shiver, and perhaps put on a jacket to warm up. If we have to go to the bathroom, we listen. Maybe that noise has to get a little louder; but ultimately, to avoid an accident, we get ourselves where we need to be.

What happens when we don't listen to the body? If you have ever been a smoker, can you think back to taking the first drag? It tasted terrible, and yet you did it anyway. In fact, it probably tasted terrible and you forced yourself into submission for whatever reason.

What about the overeater? Our body tells us when we've had enough to eat. Yet, sometimes, we just don't listen. We keep eating and eating until we need to buy bigger clothes. We feed our emotions, not our body. Then we feel as though our body betrays us by growing larger.

Sometimes our emotions try to get our attention, and we ignore them to the point that pain manifests itself into a physical symptom. This is why primary care doctors see people with physical ailments they can't find a cause for.

Storekeeper

No one really prepares us for the grief that we go through when our children grow up and start their own lives. As a mom, and especially as a single mom, I am my own storekeeper. I own my store. As my kids grow up, they create their own stores, and I become a customer in their stores. This is sometimes a hard reality to grasp.

As a parent to young children, and even teenagers, we are the supervisor of all things. As our children grow and mature, and start their own stores, we become a spectator.

We no longer have obligations to them, and we no longer have input either. We can be their cheerleaders, but the reality is we are just fans in the stand; watching. We hope for a fair call by the referees, but we aren't the players anymore. We aren't on the field, and for the most part, we sit and watch.

This is a grief that isn't talked about often and definitely not well.

Stand Strong

He who stands on tiptoe doesn't stand firm. This is the first line of a famous quote by Lao Tzu. I had a client say it to me once, and I couldn't understand what he meant. Over time, the meaning became clearer to me, and it made perfect sense. Don't we all need a strong foundation on which to do just about anything in life? If we don't have solid ground beneath us, what we are building will crumble easily.

Balance

This goes hand in hand with standing strong. We like balance. We strive for it, and we feel best when we have it. When our balance shifts, we search for coping mechanisms. The smoker grabs a cigarette, the eater gets a cookie. When we lose balance, we go to our vice or habit. If we don't have a vice or habit, we're not okay. Find ways to create balance in your life, without using negative coping skills.

Projection

This is one of those therapy terms we do use often (compared to "how does that make you feel?). Frequently, people try to force their feelings onto those around them. This is often an unconscious decision people make, but not always. Politics and religion are two places where this can easily be seen, especially in today's world. If you don't share the viewpoints that I do, then, well, you need to and here's how and why. Be mindful of your own feelings and thoughts. Feel free to share them with friends and family, and even foes, just don't push them onto others.

Crest Rider

I have already said this, but it's important to be reminded, people that you might not expect to go to therapy, actually do go to therapy. I had the privilege of providing counseling for an older gentleman who had lost his wife some years before. He had been a Pastor in his church for over 50 years. He taught me about being a crest rider.

We all have crests to ride throughout life. As we know, life isn't easy and we need support around us. Who rides with you? Who is there for you when things are going well? Who is there when things aren't going so well?

Who do you ride the crest with? Consider it a blessing, and a gift, if you can ride the crest with someone you love or care about.

Love Yourself

When someone calls for an appointment, they will give a reason why they are coming in. Whatever that reason is, it's probably true. But what most people are calling to really say is, "please help me love myself". That's the real cure we are all looking for. That's what we want — to truly love ourselves without judgment. A therapist can help you on that path.

How to Love

I have said for many years that love is an action word. Yes, it's a feeling too, but how does someone know you love them? How do you know that someone loves you? It takes action to show it. That's one of the many reasons books like *The Five Love Languages* are so popular. They take the guesswork out of how we show love.

Gary Chapman does a wonderful job of outlining how to love someone. I'm going to break it down even smaller and simpler. Affection, Attention, and Appreciation. This is what we all want and need to feel loved. Of course, it is easier said than done at times. It's a modest way of doing things. Give someone your affection, show them attention, and express your appreciation, and notice how your relationship changes for the better.

WARNING: Don't do these things with the expectation you will get something in return—that's not true love.

Ignore It

If you look straight ahead, you cannot see your nose. Go ahead and give it a try. If you close one eye and look down, yep — there's your nose! Pretty cool, huh? Your brain can ignore what is right in front of you, if it's not important. This is powerful. When something doesn't serve a purpose, or serves a negative purpose such as anxiety or depression, turn up your ability to ignore it. You can do that.

Good or Bad

Once a client said this to me, I couldn't unhear it. I wrote it down where I could see it daily; "You become what you are told — good or bad". It changed the way I responded to people sitting on the couch. I made sure, from that moment forward, to always tell them about the good they could do. I'm sure I did that before hearing this — but now I'm even more keenly aware of my words being good. I tell my clients all sorts of things they can do now, that are good, as I teach them to love themselves.

Choose to Dance

We can't always choose the music playing in our lives. However, we can choose how we dance to it. Learn to dance to whatever melody you hear. It's completely okay to march to your own drum. Just be kind, and dance like no one is watching.

Shifting Gears

Recently, my son and I exchanged cars for the week. It was unintentional, but nevertheless, it happened. His car is silver and has a stick shift (that's the extent of my knowledge of cars, by the way). As I drove his car for the week, I started recognizing that life is a lot like driving a 6 speed. It's all about balance. As you let off the clutch, you must carefully give it an appropriate amount of gas, or the engine stalls and you can't go anywhere. If you give too much gas, the engine revs, and you still go nowhere. Learn balance (and learn how to drive a stick shift — it's an important life lesson).

Should and Could

Haven't we all heard the word "should"? It's one of my least favorite words ever. I should clean the kitchen. I should go to the gym. I should stop smoking. I should lose weight. Ugh. It brings about shame and guilt, and an obligation to do something that I may not want to do, yet I feel forced to do anyway. No one likes that. In all places possible, I use the word "could" instead. It's a simple adjustment, and it makes a world of difference. I could clean the kitchen. I could go to the gym. I could stop smoking. I could lose weight. Immediately, with the word could, I feel like I am being given an opportunity and a choice. And that is always better than being forced to do something.

Live It, Own It, Act It

That line came from, where else, but a client. He was a co-dependent man in his late 40s, struggling with how to break the cycle of being dependent on strong-willed dominant women in his life. First his mother, then his wife of many years, and next his girlfriend. That became his motto: Live it, own it, act it. He began doing just that.

If you have ever wondered about the value in seeing a therapist, I would encourage you to be like Nike and just do it! Therapists are trained listeners, and not advice-givers (a common fallacy). In fact, as an intern, I had a client complain because I wouldn't tell her what to do. A good therapist will listen while you talk, and hear what you don't say, as much as what you do say.

It will sometimes seem as though what you had for dinner last night turns into your childhood trauma because a skilled therapist will gently guide you there, with seamless transitions. Many times people are afraid to seek counseling, and it can be overwhelming. In some ways, finding the right therapist is like the worst parts of dating someone new. You may find someone you think is a good fit, so you schedule the appointment. Immediately you realize it's a bad fit, and you have to move on quickly.

It's worth it to do some initial research. It's essential to have an idea of what is important to you when choosing a therapist so you can find someone that matches your criteria. It could be location, or the specialty of the therapist, or even the convenience of a telehealth modality. You might even consider asking around your friends, family, or co-workers, to see who they recommend and why.

Keep in mind that therapy is hard work, and you may start to feel worse before you start to feel better. I've had more than one person admit they didn't want to come back after a particularly difficult session, and even some who blame me for encouraging them to face their difficulties head-on (that is why they are there).

Go to your regularly scheduled appointment, even if you think you don't have anything to talk about. Some of the best sessions are the ones where the client has nothing specific they want to discuss, and yet it becomes where the deepest work is done. Even minor things can reveal larger issues, and a seasoned therapist will be able to guide you through.

The most important thing is to start the process, if you feel it is right for you. The goal is about making you better, giving you an outlet, and allowing you the opportunity to improve any area of your life. If you are unsure about why people see a therapist, refer back to Chapter 3. Self-care is not selfish, and you deserve the best life has to offer. If you don't believe that, definitely find a therapist to help you see your self-worth!

Chapter 20
Have You Ever Committed Suicide?

Back in Chapter 2, I did a pretty good job of explaining why I care, I hope. I didn't have the best childhood, and I know so many people can relate to that. Ultimately, my career choice picked me, as opposed to me picking it. My start in the field was rocky and, well, quite hilarious.

In order to obtain a Master's Degree in Social Work, I had to do a practicum or internship. Those are just fancy words for "free labor". In fact, the requirement was 512 hours of clinical work. So, essentially it was a full-time job, while also working a full-time job. As students, we were tasked with finding agencies within the community where we could get hands-on experience with real live individuals that needed mental health services.

I am fairly confident the agency expected the school to prepare us, and the school expected the agency would train us properly. I was placed in a rural area, doing community mental health counseling. The wealthiest of these folks were dirt poor, the others couldn't afford the dirt. This particular agency I was placed in had two main components. One side of the building housed a large group of individuals with severe and extreme mental illness — think Schizophrenia. The other side was for outpatient mental health counseling.

After a brief orientation and tour of the building, I was handed a stack of documents, called a biopsychosocial assessment. It was then my job to complete the intake and begin therapy. Then, my first client was led into a broom closet, also known as my office. I was absolutely terrified. I had not been given an opportunity to observe any other therapist in the agency, and there was no "real" therapist sitting in the room with me for this.

This all happened in a 2004 time frame, so I won't even begin to remember my first client's name (I couldn't share it anyway). But I do remember the look on his face. He was terrified of me. I hope my face didn't show how frightened I was as well. I went down the list of questions, asking each one on the form, and taking careful note of his answers.

Then it happened. I looked right at him, and said, "Have you ever committed suicide?" I didn't even realize what I had asked, or that I had asked it incorrectly, until he stammered and couldn't answer it.

Let me tell you — I've come a long way since that day in my broom closet!

That was the beginning of a wonderful career in mental health counseling. I have worked in various other agencies, and started a private adoption agency in two states. I have seen it and heard it all. I have worked with people who have murdered, individuals with bizarre fetishes, and people who are just there to tell me how to do my job.

For example, there was Joe and Sara. I had been seeing Joe for about a year, and he was as co-dependent as they come. He was in a relationship with a semi-retired attorney, Sara. Sara didn't feel that Joe was making enough progress, so she wanted to come into the session to discuss treatment options for Joe. Sara came with him on the scheduled day, and my administrative staff asked her to complete the standard paperwork (I had previously allowed her to come to one session as a courtesy).

Sara refused to complete the intake documents, which basically give me written permission to speak with her, so I refused to allow her into my office. As I was explaining this to her, she pulled a paper from her purse and handed it to me. She said to me, "I'm just here to make sure you do your job. Here's what Joe needs to improve on". Then she left.

I took Joe back to my office and did a termination session with him. I discussed finding him a different therapist, as we both knew that Sara wasn't going to allow him to continue seeing me since I had gone against her self-imposed policies for my office.

To my surprise, the next week, Joe returned for his regularly scheduled session and admitted he had lied to Sara about coming back. I explained to Joe that I wasn't going to be his side-chick. He had to be honest with her about keeping me as his therapist, or I would help him find another one.

As much as Sara rattled me that day (more like annoyed), there have been a couple of situations where looking back, I'm not sure I was safe. Once, I allowed someone's relative to come to my home for hypnosis to stop smoking. I was relatively new at hypnosis at the time, so I had spent quite some time getting myself ready to walk this young man into the new world as a non-smoker.

To be honest, I didn't take a thorough assessment of Mike. I incorrectly assumed that if there were any major issues, the relative would have mentioned that. Worst mistake ever for me. I should have known better.

As I began the induction, Mike looked around the room. He said he was picturing the refrigerator becoming a projectile missile, and using it as a way to have the entire house explode. I was undeterred, and I kept going with the induction. I had been taught that whatever the client says is right. The next thing Mike says is that there had been a murder in my home, he was responsible for it, and he wanted to take full responsibility and send himself to prison for it.

Okay, session is over. I abruptly ended the hypnosis before it had really even started.

I later found out that Mike was diagnosed with Schizoaffective Disorder and had stopped taking his medication months prior. Note to self — ALWAYS do an assessment and get mental health history.

I can't remember who came to me first, Mike or Sam. I saw both of them within a few months of one another. Sam was referred to my office for counseling by his insurance company. He shared that he had fantasies, dark fantasies that he knew he couldn't act on, but he wanted to.

Sam stated that he enjoyed sex with animals, children, and corpses. Now, since these were not readily available to him, he used the Dark Web to play out his fantasies. Initially, I wasn't sure if he was being truthful. I looked around my office for cameras, thinking this was a setup.

Without judgment or criticism, I asked enough detailed questions to determine that Sam was quite serious and truly interested in these things. I referred him to an addictions specialist that I trusted and knew personally. Sam agreed to see this practitioner. A few weeks later, my colleague called me. He shared that he had met with Sam, and stated that Sam was one of the most disturbed individuals he had ever met with — and he had previously worked in a men's prison. My friend was so rattled by Sam that he referred him to another specialist.

I sincerely hope Sam got the help he desperately needed and that we routed him to the best clinician to help him.

Early in my career, I began working with a local agency that assisted individuals affected by homicide. Through some state funding, I provided counseling for the families. I met with a mom who had lost her daughter, and at the time it was an unsolved murder.

I always took the time to ask about the person who died. I wanted to get to know them, so I could understand the dynamics of the relationship to better assist in grief counseling. I asked Nancy to tell me about her daughter, and she gave a long list of attributes. None of them were positive. Strange. I asked Nancy what regrets she had about her relationship with her daughter. She said she had no regrets. Again, strange from a grieving mother.

As it turns out, Nancy was arrested for her daughter's death. She had killed her daughter and tried to cover it up.

Here's what I learned as a result of working with Nancy. As a therapist, when someone confesses murder to me, I am under no obligation to report that to the authorities. If someone admits they are thinking of harming themselves or someone else, I have a duty to warn law enforcement, as well as the intended victim.

So, now I'm accepting all murder confessions? Not exactly, and it is most certainly not going to be included in my advertising.

One of the jobs that I loved the most was conducting home studies for families wanting to provide foster care to children removed from their biological families. I was able to travel to different areas of my state, and meet a wide variety of people. You can learn a lot by going into someone's home. One of the questions we had to ask was about gun safety.

One particular home I visited was out in the country — to put it mildly. Grandma and Grandpa were trying to get their home approved to care for their grandchildren, ages 6 and 8. I asked my standard questions about whether or not a gun was kept in the home.

Grandpa explained that he kept one gun under his pillow and another one on the front seat of his pickup truck. I asked the next logical question…. "Are the guns loaded in these locations?" He looked me straight in the eye and said, "Darlin', if it ain't loaded, it ain't no good".

Home study denied.

Being a social worker is a lot like how Forrest Gump compared life to a box of chocolates. You never know what you're going to get. Some days you're the windshield, and some days you are the bug. Some days you save the world, and other days the world attacks you.

Chances are seeing your therapist is pretty tame in comparison to these stories. Your therapist thanks you for the mild story you bring to his/her office.

Chapter 21
It's a Wrap!

So you've finished the book. How did it make you feel? Joking, we never ask that, but it is my hope that you thought, and felt, many things as you went through what I wrote. I hope I challenged you. I hope I challenged, and maybe changed, what you think of therapy, and, of course, therapists. But, most importantly, I hope it gave you a chance to think about yourself, who you are, who you want to be, and what steps you might take to become that person. Oh, and I hope you laughed.

I shared a lot about myself. I know some of that was not pleasant, but I wanted you to see who I am, and where I come from. I wanted you to see why I chose a career in therapy, and not school teaching (though I have the highest respect for school teachers). I wanted you to see me as a person; therapists are people too. I hope, too, that you can see from my story that we can overcome our past. The traumas we've been through don't have to be who we are. We can't change the past, but we can change how we let it control us.

Also, I wanted to talk about myself because it's therapeutic. That's what therapy is. It's that one chance you get to just be yourself, unjudged, and just talk about yourself. Therapy is at its best when you allow yourself to really be you, to see yourself in that mirror. To really see yourself, be yourself, express who you really are, is a powerful tool. Before we can change, we must know who we are, who we really are. The first step to change is understanding.

People who seek therapy are not "crazy". Okay, I've met some people who have certainly had issues with reality, but the vast majority of my clients are not like that. People come to therapy because they have things in their life they need help with. I know nothing about cars, so I would see a mechanic if I needed help with my car. The difference between a therapist and a mechanic is that a mechanic does some sort of magic I don't see and then charges me, whereas a therapist works directly with you. In the end, the change comes from within you, as the therapist guides you in your understanding. Remember, we don't give advice, we don't tell you what to do, and we help you find what you want to do.

I gave you a list of ten reasons to talk to a therapist in Chapter 3. I'm not going to tell you all that again (if you've forgotten, go and read it again). What I want to say is; therapy is good. Simple as that. Now you're thinking, she's a therapist – of course she'd say that. True enough, but remember the statistics; 59 million people have received mental health treatment in the last two years, and 80% of those report it was effective. I haven't checked, but I'd say that's even better than chocolate (or maybe not). It works, and I really believe we have to remove the stigma from seeing a therapist. Remember, therapists see therapists.

I think one of the things that stops many people from attending therapy is the fear. There is fear of what happens in therapy, fear of what a therapist might be like, and fear of what facing up to yourself might be like. I'd like to think that this book has helped with that. Therapists are people. We are not perfect, and we don't think we are – at least the successful ones don't. We are listeners, good listeners, who are focused on you. You really can tell us anything, we listen and guide. We don't judge.

Therapy itself is not scary. Yes, sometimes clients cry, but they also laugh. Laughter in therapy is more common than you might imagine, and it's good. Therapy brings out strong emotions, but they are there for a reason. It's better to cry in a supportive environment than to keep that feeling stuck inside you. And, it's always good to laugh. Every session is unique, because every client is unique. In all of my years, I only had two sessions that were quite uncomfortable for me. (I mentioned those earlier).

This book is not an advertisement for me, or for my private practice. This is simply intended to give you a better idea of what we, therapists, are like and do. Maybe you have some issues you'd like to discuss, something you want to talk about, but feel uncomfortable opening up about with friends or family. If so, I hope you will consider seeing a therapist.

Therapy is not being weak. In fact, attending therapy is a demonstration of strength. Making a decision to see a therapist is making a decision to take action, to face your issues, and to take a big step forward in your journey of self-development.

Yes, change can be hard. Yes, facing who you really are, seeing yourself in that unvarnished mirror, can be difficult. But, you can do it. We are, each of us, much stronger than we think. We can face our trauma, our grief, and move to a place where it no longer dominates us. Yes, we may need help to do that, but it's just that – help. The real power, the real strength, comes from within you. When you understand yourself, when you can see the path better, then you can be that person who you really want to be.

When you think of my past, don't be sad for me. Be happy that I have been able to move beyond that. It no longer controls me. I did it, just a girl from Alabama. You can do it too! I needed some help along the way, maybe you could use some help too. Please get comfortable allowing someone to journey with you. It's worth it. Be that crest rider.

You are Invited!

Dr. Tracy Riley is available for counseling, conversation, and continuing education for your group.

Visit her website at www.tracyriley.com or call (904) 704-2527 to book her today.

Check out her other books:
https://www.tracyriley.com/books

Your Call to Action

Thank you for reading Tales From The Couch: Healing, Humor, and Finding Hope!

I greatly appreciate all of your feedback, and I love hearing what you have to say—and being on the journey with you.

Your input helps to make the next version of this book and future projects even better.

Please share a thoughtful 5 star review on Amazon letting me know how much you enjoyed the book.

Thank you so much.

Check out my other books:
https://www.tracyriley.com/books

- Dr. Tracy Riley

www.ingramcontent.com/pod-product-compliance
Lightning Source LLC
LaVergne TN
LVHW051522070426
8355071LV00023B/3260